I OUGHT TO BE IN PICTURES

I OUGHT TO BE IN PICTURES

A New Comedy by

Neil Simon

Random House New York

Library of Congress Cataloging in Publication Data

Simon, Neil.
  Neil Simon's I ought to be in pictures.

  I. Title. II. Title: I ought to be in pictures.
PS3537.I663I15   812'.54   80–6048
ISBN 0-394-51774-1

To my mother and father

I OUGHT TO BE IN PICTURES *was first presented on January 17, 1980, at the Mark Taper Forum, Los Angeles, with the following cast:*

LIBBY TUCKER	Dinah Manoff
STEFFY BLONDELL	Joyce Van Patten
HERB TUCKER	Tony Curtis

Directed by Herbert Ross

Scenery by David Jenkins

Lighting by Tharon Musser

Costumes by Nancy Potts

I OUGHT TO BE IN PICTURES *was first presented in New York City on April 3, 1980, at the Eugene O'Neill Theatre, with the following cast:*

LIBBY TUCKER	Dinah Manoff
STEFFY BLONDELL	Joyce Van Patten
HERB TUCKER	Ron Leibman

Directed by Herbert Ross

Scenery by David Jenkins

Lighting by Tharon Musser

Costumes by Nancy Potts

Synopsis of Scenes

Act One

Act Two

Act I

SCENE 1

*The scene is a small bungalow in West Hollywood. It is a
rather colorless affair with cheap, rundown furniture. There
is a small kitchen off the living room, a small bedroom and
one tiny bathroom. A door leads to a small backyard, with
three trees.*

*As the curtain rises, it is about nine o'clock in the morning,
a bright, sunny California morning. The radio is playing. A
young girl, short, about twenty, wearing sawed-off jeans,
sweat socks, hiking boots, a back-pack, an army jacket, a
beret, and carrying an old valise stands outside the door. Her
name is* LIBBY TUCKER. *She has an energy and a vitality that
will soon make themselves apparent.*

STEFFY BLONDELL, *a still-attractive woman close to forty
is in the bathroom combing her hair.*

LIBBY *rings the front doorbell.* STEFFY *turns off the radio,
goes to the door and opens it.*

STEFFY Yes?

LIBBY Hi!

STEFFY Hi! Can I help you? *surprise at confidence*

LIBBY *(Looks into the room)* I don't know. I'm not sure
this is the place.

STEFFY Who are you looking for?

LIBBY Does Herbert Tucker live here?

STEFFY Yes, he does.

3

LIBBY   Which Herbert Tucker is he?

STEFFY   I didn't know there were a lot of them. Which one are you looking for?
(She picks up a newspaper from the front steps)

LIBBY   Is this the Herbert Tucker in show business?

STEFFY   Yes . . .

LIBBY   He's a writer?

STEFFY   Yes. What did you want?
(She comes back inside)

LIBBY   I wanted to talk to him. Is he in?

STEFFY   He's sleeping. Listen, I'm kind of busy. Could you tell me what this is about?

LIBBY   It's personal . . . Are you his wife?

STEFFY   No, I'm not . . . Are you a friend of his?

LIBBY   No. I'm his daughter.
(There is a pause. STEFFY looks taken aback)

STEFFY   His *daughter*?

LIBBY   Libby. Libby Tucker. From New York City.

STEFFY   I see.

LIBBY   I think I stunned you.

STEFFY   No, not at all.

LIBBY   A little, right?

STEFFY   Yes, a little . . . Please come in. Sit down.
(LIBBY comes in, puts her bag down)   He didn't mention you were coming.

4

LIBBY   That's because he didn't know. Is this like his office or something?

STEFFY   Well, both. He works here and he lives here.

LIBBY   I see.

STEFFY   It's not what you expected?

LIBBY   I don't know. You get this picture in your mind about Hollywood. I live this good in Brooklyn.

STEFFY   He usually has a woman come in and clean it a couple of times a week.

LIBBY   Couldn't make it this week, huh?

STEFFY   I don't know. *quickly* I'm not here that often.

LIBBY   Oh. You don't live here?

STEFFY   *quickly* No. *(Extending her hand)* My name is Steffy Blondell.

LIBBY   Glad to meet you, Steffy Blondell.
   (They shake hands)

STEFFY   Are you just out for a visit?

LIBBY   *(Looking around)*   No. I'm sort of out on business.

STEFFY   I see. Can I get you anything?

LIBBY   A glass of water would be swell. I think I swallowed the state of Arizona.

STEFFY   *(Going to the sink)*   Wouldn't you like to take that thing off?

LIBBY   What thing?

STEFFY   That pack on your back.

LIBBY   Oh, Jeez, I forgot it was still there.   *(She takes it off)*   After you carry it for three weeks, you think it's a growth.

STEFFY   He should be up in a few minutes. I hate to wake him. He hasn't been sleeping too well lately.
(She hands her the glass)

LIBBY   Yeah? Is he all right?

STEFFY   Oh, sure. Just a little rundown.

LIBBY   All his various multiple projects, I suppose.
(She drinks)

STEFFY   Well, he keeps busy.

LIBBY   *(Winces)*   Jesus, is this water? You could eat it with a spoon.

STEFFY   It probably tastes funny after the water in New York. He really should get a filter.

LIBBY   And a fishing pole.

STEFFY   That's something *he* would say. You sound a lot like him.

LIBBY   You mean the *Noo Yawk* accent?

STEFFY   No. Just the way you say things. I think you have his sense of humor.

LIBBY   Well, that's about all he left.
(She looks around)

STEFFY   You're not in school then, I take it.

LIBBY   You mean college? No.

6

STEFFY   Because your father mentioned a few weeks ago he thought you might be in college by now.

LIBBY   He's not exactly up on my current activities, is he? No, I just missed getting into Harvard by about three million kids . . . I'm an actress.

STEFFY   Really?

LIBBY   Yeah.

STEFFY   You mean professional?

LIBBY   Yeah. Sorta professional. I mean, I'm not a star. If I was a star you would have known who I was when I said "Libby Tucker."

STEFFY   What do you do, stage work mostly?

LIBBY   No, mostly I audition.

STEFFY   But you have studied.

LIBBY   You mean in acting school? No. I never had the time or the money. I had a part-time job in the notions department in Abraham and Straus. I was *almost* accepted for a scholarship at the Actors Studio.

STEFFY   What happened?

LIBBY   Nothing. They just didn't accept me.

STEFFY   I see. So you just decided to come. I mean, you didn't write or anything?

LIBBY   Yeah. When I was nine . . . He answered when I was twelve. *(Looking around)* Just one bedroom?

STEFFY   Yes. I was just about to go out shopping. Your father's not very good about keeping his refrigerator filled.

7

LIBBY   You don't have to go on my account. I mean, that
water was a meal in itself.

STEFFY   If I don't do it, he never will. It's just down the
block.

LIBBY   You know him long?

STEFFY   About two years. We date on and off.

LIBBY   Two years and you just see him "on and off"?

STEFFY   Well, I work and I raise two children. It's difficult.

LIBBY   Yeah, I know. My mother has the same problem.
(STEFFY *lets that pass*)   So what's he like?

STEFFY   You mean you have no idea?

LIBBY   No.

STEFFY   I'm sorry. *apologize for my blunder*

LIBBY   It's no big deal. I'm okay. I came very close to
growing up neurotic but I got over it.

touch her

STEFFY   I'm glad . . . Your mother raised you?

LIBBY   (*Raises her hand waist-high*)   Up to here. The
rest I did myself. Mom was working all the time and
she had my brother Robby to take care of. Actually,
my mother and my father was my grandmother.
Grandma gave me a sense of direction. She gave me
confidence in myself. I'm sure you noticed my confidence. It's the one thing about me you can't miss.

STEFFY   I noticed it the minute you said "Hi" . . . How'd
you get out here?

LIBBY   I took the bus to Denver, then I hitchhiked. If you're not gorgeous, you hike more than you hitch. Listen, it wasn't bad. I got to see America, they got to see me. We both made a big impression.

STEFFY   Maybe I should wake him up, huh? Tell him you're here.

LIBBY   No, that's okay. I sort of have it all planned in my mind what I wanna say. I can handle it.

STEFFY   I was worrying how *he's* going to handle it.

LIBBY   Oh, you mean the shock? He doesn't have a bad heart, does he?

STEFFY   No.

LIBBY   Maybe I should slide a note under his door first.

STEFFY   Listen, he'll be fine. Maybe I just worry about him too much.

LIBBY   I don't even know what he looks like. I've never even seen a picture of him. I don't even know what to call him.

STEFFY   You don't know what to call him?

LIBBY   Well, he isn't exactly "Poppa" and I don't think "Mr. Tucker" is gonna win him over. *hug her*

STEFFY   Look, if it's a problem, just tell him. He'll understand. He's really a nice man, you know.

LIBBY   Really? Like, what's nice about him?

STEFFY   Well, why don't you wait. Make up your own mind.

9

LIBBY   That's what Grandma told me to do last week at the cemetery.

STEFFY   Someone died?

LIBBY   Yeah. Grandma. About six years ago. But I go out there every few weeks to talk to her.

STEFFY   I'm not sure I understand.

LIBBY   I know. It sounds weird. When I told my mother Grandma still talks to me, she wanted me to take laxatives . . . It's hard to explain to most people. But I sort of always depended on Grandma. And when I need her the most, somehow she gets through to me. (STEFFY *stares at her*) You're looking at me funny. I swear I'm not one of those people who sees miracles. This isn't *The Song of Bernadette* or anything.

STEFFY   No, I think I know what you're saying.

LIBBY   She tells me if I'm eating too much or not getting enough sleep. Last week she didn't have much to say because she just had a fight with Grandpa. He's in the grave next to her.

STEFFY   Does he talk to you too?

LIBBY   He doesn't talk to Grandma, why should he talk to me?

STEFFY   I'll tell you the truth, it's something I've always wanted to do myself. Just go to the cemetery and talk to my mother, tell her what's going on with my life. But I always felt foolish.
   (*She goes to the telephone and dials*)

LIBBY   Oh, don't I know. I had a girlfriend sleep over
one night and three o'clock in the morning I had this
conversation with Grandma. My friend didn't even
stay for breakfast.

STEFFY   *(Into the phone)*   Three-seven-seven. Did the
studio call for me?

LIBBY   Are you in the business too?

STEFFY   Mm-hm. Make-up lady. I work over at Columbia.

LIBBY   Columbia Pictures? The movie studio? I'm having heart palpitations.

STEFFY   *(Into the phone)*   If the studio calls, tell them I'll
be in at ten-thirty. Thank you.
    (STEFFY *hangs up*)

LIBBY   Who do you make up? Any actual stars?

STEFFY   Sure.

LIBBY   Sure, she says. Like I have this conversation every
day. Name me one star. A big one. Who was the big-
gest?

STEFFY   I don't know . . . Jane Fonda?

LIBBY   JANE FONDA? *You've touched Jane Fonda's
face?* I mean, Jane Fonda is the one actress in the world
I most identify with. I patterned my whole life after
hers. I feel I have so many of her qualities. They just
haven't surfaced yet.

STEFFY   Well, one day if you're not busy you can come
out to the studio, I'll show you around.

(STEFFY *picks up her purse and goes to the front porch*)

LIBBY (*Following after* STEFFY) What do you mean, if I'm not busy? How many phone calls have I got since I'm here?

touch her shoulder

STEFFY It's no problem. I'll set it up.

LIBBY God's truth: I liked your face the minute I saw it through the door. Maybe I should forget my old man and move in with you.

a bit worry

STEFFY Is that what you're planning to do? Move in with him?

LIBBY I don't know. Let's see if I get a handshake first. (STEFFY *stands on the doorstoop pondering* LIBBY's *last remark as* LIBBY *goes into the house and closes the front door.* STEFFY *leaves.* LIBBY *looks around the room, then sits down. The telephone rings. She looks at the bedroom door, then rushes to answer it to avoid waking her father. Into the phone*) Hello? . . . Who? Oh, er . . . No. He's sleeping . . . No, this is er—sort of his daughter . . . Yeah. Sure I know how to take a message. (*Picks up a pencil*) Wait a minute. I need a piece of paper. (*She starts to look through the mess on the desk. She finally finds paper in the top drawer. Into the phone*) Okay. Go ahead . . . "Stan Marx called. You got a turndown at NBC. Do you want to try CBS again?" Is that it? . . . Yeah, I got it . . . You're welcome. Goodbye. (LIBBY *hangs up. The bedroom door opens. A sleepy-eyed* HERB TUCKER *comes out in his pajama bottoms and an old T-shirt. He heads right for the coffee. She turns and notices him*) Oh! Hi!

HERB (*Doesn't look at her*) I didn't hear you get up.

LIBBY   That's because I didn't sleep here.

HERB   *(Looks at her)*   I thought you were Steffy.   *(He calls out)   Steffy!*

LIBBY   She went shopping.

HERB   Steffy did?

LIBBY   Yeah.

HERB   Who are you?

LIBBY   Libby.

HERB   You're the cleaning girl today, Libby?

LIBBY   No. Just Libby.

HERB   Steffy's niece.

LIBBY   No.

HERB   Come on, kid. It's too early. Don't play games with me. Libby who?

LIBBY   Libby Tucker.

HERB   *(No reaction)*   Libby *Tucker?*

LIBBY   Libby Gladyce Tucker . . . Blanche's girl?

HERB   What are you saying to me?

LIBBY   I'm saying, I'm your daughter. I didn't mean to sneak up on you like this. It must be an awful shock, heh?

HERB   Yeah. A little. A little . . . Could you wait one second? Let me get a little coffee down.
    (He pours coffee and sips some)

LIBBY I suppose I should have called first, but it seemed harder to say over the phone than in person . . . Are you okay?

HERB I'm fine. I'm fine. I just want to get a little more coffee down.
(He drinks some more)

LIBBY I got out here yesterday, so I thought I'd just come by and look you up.

HERB You looked me up, heh?

LIBBY I found your address in the telephone book.

HERB Looked it up in the telephone book, heh?

LIBBY Uh-huh . . . This is coming at you a little fast, isn't it?

HERB Yeah, a little. This is really terrific . . . Where's what's-her-name?

LIBBY Steffy?

HERB Steffy. Where did she go?

LIBBY Shopping. She'll be right back. She went to get breakfast.

HERB Oh, that's too bad. I wanted her to meet you.

LIBBY We met.

HERB Where do you know Steffy from?

LIBBY From the door. She opened it and I came in.

HERB Oh, I see. Just now.

LIBBY When I came to look you up.

HERB   Okay, I got it. I got it. I'm up now . . . Jesus, what a surprise. Don't you feel like that?

LIBBY   No. I knew I was coming.

HERB   When did you decide all this?

LIBBY   About two years ago. That's how long it took me to save the money to come out here.

HERB   This is really incredible. I was just talking about you the other day to . . . what's-her-name?

LIBBY   Steffy?

HERB   To Steffy. I suddenly can't remember anybody's name. I'm sorry. I'm a little fuzzy. I took a sleeping pill about an hour ago.

LIBBY   An hour ago?

HERB   I like to wait until the last minute, in case I fall asleep on my own. Would you wait one second? *(He goes to the sink and dashes water on his face)* Listen, could you pull down that window shade? It really bothers me.

LIBBY   You don't like the sun?

HERB   Not every day for sixteen years.

LIBBY   I love this kind of weather. Although I hear it rains a lot out here.
        (She pulls down the shade)

HERB   Thirty inches of rain in two hours. The rest of the year is all sun.

LIBBY   I thought I'd find you all sunburned.

HERB   I hate it. It tries to get at me through the cracks in the door. I gotta hide.

LIBBY   Listen, after all those winters in New York, this is terrific.

HERB   Oh, well, this is temporary. I'm moving. I got a nice place picked out up in the Hollywood Hills. I'm supposed to move in a few weeks. I just gotta wait for a couple of things to come through.

LIBBY   What kind of things?

HERB   Oh, things. In the business. I got a very big deal on the fire right now. You wouldn't understand.

LIBBY   *(Picks up the message)*   Oh. There was a message for you. Stan Marx called. He said you got a turndown from NBC. Did you want to try CBS again?

HERB   Oh.   *(He looks at the message)*   Yeah, well, this wasn't important . . . This wasn't the deal I was talking about . . . You have a very nice handwriting. You make *w*'s like I do.

LIBBY   *(Proud)*   Yeah? I guess I inherited that, huh?

HERB   Jesus, I can't get over how grown up you've got. Turn around. Let me look at you.

LIBBY   This is it. I don't get any bigger.

HERB   You don't have to. You're perfect.

LIBBY   I'm a shrimp.

HERB   You're petite. I wouldn't want you any bigger. And you've got plenty of time to grow yet . . . How old are you now?

LIBBY   I was nineteen on my last birthday.

HERB *Nineteen?* Already? Can you believe that?

LIBBY Yeah. *I* can.

HERB It was in December, wasn't it? December thirteenth, fourteenth . . .

LIBBY July fifth.

HERB July fifth. Of course. I remember that day. I was at the ball game. I just got home. Yankees–Red Sox. Yankees won it five-three in the bottom of the tenth. Hank Bauer hit a homer with Berra on second with one out.

LIBBY Boy, you sure remember birthdays good.

HERB And now you're this regular beautiful young lady.

LIBBY Well, not so beautiful.

HERB Of course you are. Who said you weren't beautiful?

LIBBY Well, nobody ever said I *was.*

HERB What do you mean? *I* just said it.

LIBBY Well, that doesn't count. You're my father.

HERB Yeah, but that was a long time ago.

LIBBY Well, thank you. I'm glad you think I'm beautiful.

HERB Very pretty. Healthy-looking, you know what I mean?

LIBBY Yeah—fat!

HERB You're not fat. You're . . . solid.

LIBBY   Same thing. Solid is hard fat.

HERB   Well, listen, you think what you want to think. I think you're beautiful. Jesus, look how I'm sitting here —in dirty pajamas. I mean, this is an important moment. I should put on a blazer or something.
(He puts on an old jacket)

LIBBY   Listen, I'm a little embarrassed . . .

HERB   Embarrassed? By what?

LIBBY   Well, I don't know what to call you.

HERB   You don't know what to call your father? Your own father? . . . You call me Herb, that's what you call your father.

LIBBY   Herb?

HERB   I mean, if you want to call me Pop or Dad, that's fine. I just didn't know how you felt about it. It's been a long time . . . But Herb is perfectly fine.

LIBBY   Okay, Herb. So isn't it time we shook hands or something? I mean, we're on a first-name basis. What do you think?

HERB   What do you mean, shake hands? Let me give you a kiss, for chrissakes. *(She steps forward eagerly. He takes her shoulders and kisses her on the side of her head. She is clearly disappointed. She moves away)* So how's your mother?

LIBBY   She's fine.

HERB   She never got married or anything?

LIBBY   No. She went with Mr. Slotkin, the butcher from Food Fair, for a couple of years. He was nice—he would bring over lamb chops, veal cutlets, things like that.

HERB   So what happened? Nothing serious?

LIBBY   No. When he started bringing over chicken wings, we knew the romance was over.

HERB   And how's Carl?

LIBBY   Who?

HERB   Carl. Your brother.

LIBBY   You mean Robby?

HERB   What do you mean, Robby? His name is Carl.

LIBBY   Not that I ever heard.

HERB   Of course. He was named after Carl Hubbell, the greatest screwball pitcher in the history of the National League.

LIBBY   Well, he shoulda spoken up. He thinks his name is Robert.

HERB   She changed his name? A beautiful name like Carl?

LIBBY   Well, you haven't seen him. He doesn't look like a Carl. He's kind of roly-poly like a Robert.

HERB   You know why, don't you? Because she hated baseball. Used to curse me every time I went out to a game. What—is that such a terrible thing, to want to go out to a baseball game? It's the most beautiful sport ever created by man.

LIBBY   You like the name Libby?

HERB   Sure I like Libby. I've always loved the name Libby.

LIBBY   What player was I named after?

HERB   You were named after my mother. You never saw her. She died before you were born . . . So what does Robby do? He goes to school?

LIBBY   Yeah.

HERB   Is he a jock? Is he a good ballplayer?

LIBBY   No. He plays piano.

HERB   The piano? He doesn't like to play ball?

LIBBY   He doesn't want to hurt his fingers.

HERB   He could play *soft* ball.

LIBBY   Once in a while he plays Ping-Pong.

HERB   Yeah? Is he any good?

LIBBY   He beat Grandma once.

HERB   Not exactly the *Wide World of Sports.* *(She's been munching on crackers)* Hey! What are you eating crackers for? I got fresh fruit here. I grow my own oranges. I have my own tree in the back. *(He takes an orange out of a basket, flips it to her)* Comin' at ya! *(She catches it)* Hey! Nice catch. Maybe *you're* the ballplayer in the family . . . Go on, taste that. *(She bites into it)* Juicy, isn't it?

LIBBY   You need a bathing suit to eat it.

HERB   Would you come here? I want you to see this. *(They go outside)* You see that? That's my orange tree.

I grew that. I planted it. I fed it. I grew it. That's *my* tree.

LIBBY   I thought only God could make a tree.

HERB   That's back East. Out here, anyone can do it . . . And that's my lemon tree. I never thought I could do things like that. I grew up on the streets of New York. I used to play stickball and now I grow lemons and oranges.

LIBBY   What's the one next to it?

HERB   That one's a pain in the ass. It grows pits with no fruit. I didn't grow that one. It came with the house. Trees are like people. If they know you don't care about them, they're not going to give you anything back.

LIBBY   Yeah . . . I know a lot of people like that.
(He looks at her, getting the point of her irony)

HERB   *(Brightly)* So what are you doing? Just visiting here? A holiday or something? Please sit. Where are you staying?

LIBBY   Last night I stayed at a motel. The Casa Valentino. You gotta use toilet paper for towels.

HERB   Well, that's crazy. I got room in here. Why don't you stay with me while you're out here?

LIBBY   I couldn't.

HERB   And I don't want to hear any back talk.

LIBBY   It's impossible. No.

HERB   It's settled. All right?

LIBBY   Sure. Thanks.

HERB   How long are you going to be out here?

LIBBY   The rest of my life.

HERB   *(Looks at her. Smiles)*   What do you mean?

LIBBY   Well, it depends on how my career goes.

HERB   What career is that?

LIBBY   I want to be in pictures.

HERB   You want to be in *what*?

LIBBY   Pictures. Movies. I'm not ruling out television, but movies are my real goal.

HERB   I see . . . Movies, heh. Well, you sure picked a tough business.

LIBBY   So did you and you seem to be doing okay.
(She looks around, realizing what she has said)

HERB   What would you do?

LIBBY   Act!

HERB   Act? You want to be an *actress*? In the *movies*? That takes a little something called talent, you know.

LIBBY   I've got talent. I've got plenty of talent. Some people think I'm kind of a female Dustin Hoffman.

HERB   What people?

LIBBY   Robby and Grandma.

HERB   Where have you ever acted?

LIBBY   Places.

HERB   What places?

LIBBY   Erasmus High School. We did *The Prime of Miss Jean Brodie.*

HERB   Really? What part did you play?

LIBBY   I didn't have a part. I was the understudy.

HERB   For Jean Brodie?

LIBBY   No. One of the girls in her class. Sandy.

HERB   Sandy? I see . . . Did you ever get on?

LIBBY   No. We only did two performances. And I had to work the lights.

HERB   Oh. You were the lighting girl.

LIBBY   *Assistant* lighting girl.

HERB   I see. So you were the assistant lighting girl who was the understudy to Sandy, for two performances of *The Prime of Miss Jean Brodie* at Erasmus Hall High School.

LIBBY   The summer session.

HERB   The summer session. Well, it's not exactly what I would call a *wealth* of experience.

LIBBY   No, it isn't. It's what you might call a "humble beginning." All I know is I believe in myself.

HERB   That's terrific. That's very important. Unfortunately, in this business everybody *else* believes in themselves . . . What are you going to do when they ask you for a résumé?

LIBBY   A what?

HERB   A résumé. A list of your credits. What you've done. I don't think it's enough to give them a picture of you working the lights at Erasmus High School.

LIBBY   I can read for them, can't I? I have this book of one-act plays that I read in my room every day. And I'm good too. I mean *really* good. Sometimes I even make myself cry. I *have* talent, I just need the outlet.

HERB   And you picked the *movies* as your outlet?

LIBBY   Yes. Because one thing I have is determination and confidence. Like, I have this tiny little flame burning deep inside of me, and I just need somebody to turn the gas jet up a little.

HERB   And who did you figure would do that?

LIBBY   I don't know. Someone out here. Someone in the business. Someone like a director—or a writer. Someone who's willing to give a young unknown kid from Brooklyn a chance.

HERB   *(Nods)*   Does he have to be from this particular neighborhood?

LIBBY   I didn't say it was you.

HERB   I was just asking.

LIBBY   But if for any reason, you should want to make a phone call on my behalf, not out of any sense of loyalty or obligation or guilt, but just because you recognize some potential in me, I would appreciate it.

HERB   Who taught you to talk like that?

LIBBY   Like what?

HERB   Like coming around corners, going up over the roof, down into the basement and coming up through the sewer. You got something to say to me, say it straight out.

LIBBY   Okay. Ordinarily I wouldn't be caught dead asking you for a favor, but it so happens that you owe me.

HERB   I what?

LIBBY   You owe me. You owe me for a lot. And Grandma said to me, "Go out to California and make sure that he pays you."

HERB   Oh, really. Is that what your grandmother told you?

LIBBY   Three weeks ago at Mount Hebron Cemetery.

HERB   What were you doing there?

LIBBY   That's where she lives. I mean, she's dead, but that's where she's buried. Next to Grandpa.

HERB   She died? I didn't know that. I'm sorry. When did this happen?

LIBBY   Six years ago, June fourteenth.

HERB   So when did you talk to her?

LIBBY   Last week.

HERB   Last *week*?

LIBBY   Last month. Last night. This morning. It's a little complicated.

HERB   I imagine it would be.

LIBBY   Forget Grandma. I'll explain it to you some other time. This is just me, Libby, the daughter you haven't seen in sixteen years asking you for a simple favor. Are you interested in helping me launch my career or not? Is that *straight* enough for you?

HERB   Hey, slow down! Slow down, will you? I've got a lot to digest here. I just found out my son Carl is called Robby, my ex-wife dated a man who brought her chicken wings and my daughter talks to her dead grandmother. Let me catch up with all the news.

LIBBY   Look, if you don't want me to stay here, just say so. I didn't come here looking for any handouts.

HERB   Jesus! You are really something. Talking to you is like a two-hour workout in the gym. Why don't you just cool off, take that chip off your shoulder and sit down? *(She glares at him)*   Will you please sit down! *Please* sit down! *(She sits)*   Now, can we start this entire morning right from the beginning again? Like you just walked in the door? Can we say hello to each other like average American people? . . . Hello.

LIBBY   *(Still uptight)*   Hello.

HERB   Thank you. Can I get you something to drink?

LIBBY   No, thanks. I just *ate* a glass of water.

HERB   Look, about this movie business. Can we discuss it a little later? I really don't like being pressured into things. You understand?

LIBBY   Well, I'm sorry if I made any *demands* on you. I won't do it again. It only comes *up* once every sixteen years.

HERB *(Glares at her)* You don't *look* like your mother but you sure *talk* like her.

LIBBY That's a crappy thing to say. Leave her out of this. My mother wasn't the one who walked out.

HERB You're right. I'm sorry. I apologize.

LIBBY Listen, I really think I better get out of here. This isn't turning out how I planned it at all. You're not what I expected, you know what I mean?

HERB No. I don't. I'm sorry if I'm a major disappointment to you. Maybe you had some image in your mind about what a father should look like and talk like, but I'm just plain old Herb Tucker, not somebody on *The Waltons.*

LIBBY I didn't mean that. I just thought you'd be a little friendlier. A little more "supportive."

HERB Why don't you give someone a chance? Why don't we get to know each other instead of just barging in here and telling me I've got to get you into the movies.

LIBBY You don't have to get me into anything. I couldn't even get a lousy kiss from you, so I sure as hell don't expect a phone call to your studio friends, because from the looks of this place, you don't got their number . . . And I don't have to get to know you because I know *everything* about you. Momma's been telling it to me since I was three years old. But I'm not interested. That's between you and her. I did fine without you. And I can manage on my own now too. You don't want to help me, swell. I happen to know people over at Columbia Pictures.

HERB   Like who?

LIBBY   Like Steffy Blondell . . . And you can keep your homemade oranges. I like mine from Florida.

HERB   You're a fresh kid, you know that?

LIBBY   And what are you? You make fun of your own daughter because she talks to her dead grandmother. I may be ditsy but I'm not the one with the tree that grows pits.

HERB   Look, I don't care how you talk in your own house, but you change that tone of voice to me. I will not be talked to that way.

LIBBY   I'll talk to you any way I please.

HERB   Not to your father, you won't.

LIBBY   My father? You're the last one in the world who's my father. My *grandmother's* my father. Boy oh boy, sixteen years of dreams down the toilet.
        (STEFFY *enters and stands there, listening*)

HERB   Who asked you to come? What is this, your mother's revenge? Do I get Robby and his piano tomorrow?

LIBBY   Grandma was right again. I should have listened to her. "Once a shitheel, always a shitheel," she told me.

HERB   That's how your grandmother talks to you?

LIBBY   The language is mine, the wisdom is hers . . . I must have been nuts. Three thousand miles and all I get is a glass of mud.

STEFFY   I hate to interrupt but you can hear this in the supermarket.

LIBBY *(To her father)* Well, let me tell you something, Mr. Herbert Tucker. The one who hasn't made it in show business is you, not me. I'm on the way up on the local and you're on the way-down express. It's possible, just possible, that one day I may be standing up there getting my Emmy Award or my Grammy or my Oscar or whatever the hell they get out here. And I'm going to smile and say to the entire world, "I want to thank everyone who helped me win this award. My grandmother, my mother, my brother Robby, my friends, my fans and everyone else except my shitheel father. I think that about covers it!" . . . I apologize for my language, Steffy. It was very nice meeting you. I'm sorry I can't say that for everyone else in this house.
(She starts for the door. HERB *catches her)*

HERB *(Angrily)* Wait a minute, you! You just listen to me a minute. I never figured I had anything coming to me. I gave you up, that was *my* loss. I left that house because if I had stayed it would have turned into a war zone and there would have been *no* survivors. You want to talk about guilts, regrets—I got enough to fill up my garage. But that's my business and I'll handle it my own way. I never expected anything from you *or* your brother. Outside this house, you can call me any goddamn thing you want to call me. But under this roof is my domain, and if you talk to me, you show me some respect.
(He walks away from her. She picks up her bag, walks out the door and then yells in)

LIBBY *(Shouts)* I am now outside—and you are still a shitheel! Goodbye, Mr. Herbert Tucker!!
(She starts to walk away)

STEFFY   Libby, wait! Wait, please!
(*She goes out after her*)

HERB   Where does she get a *mouth* like that?   (*He heads for his bedroom*)   Crazy! That whole family was crazy from the minute I met them.
(*He goes in and slams the door*)

STEFFY   (*Catches* LIBBY)   Libby, don't go. Not like this. Please. Come on back in.

LIBBY   (*On the verge of tears*)   He didn't even listen. He just thinks I came out here to get something from him. Well, he doesn't have anything I want.

STEFFY   You can't expect everything to happen in ten minutes. Give the man some time.

LIBBY   And then he makes some cracks about my mother. I don't have to listen to cracks about my mother . . . And he doesn't know everything about show business. Tells me I have to have a résumé. Well, my "résumé" is a lot better than the "telephone messages" he gets. I'm glad you think he's worth it, but maybe that's because you don't happen to be the daughter he walked out on.
(*She runs off.* STEFFY *watches her, then turns and goes back into the house. She starts for the kitchen, when* HERB *comes out of his bedroom. He has put on slacks and a shirt. They look at each other, silently.* STEFFY *starts to unpack the grocery bag*)

HERB   Hell of a way to wake up.

STEFFY   I wanted to tell you she was here. But she wanted to surprise you. She had it all planned out what she was going to say.

HERB   You mean she's been *working* on that speech?

STEFFY   What happened, Herb?

HERB   *(After a pause)*   She tells me I'm not what she expected . . . A strange kid walks in here in a mountain-climbing outfit, talks like Marlon Brando, tells me she was sent out here by her dead grandmother in Brooklyn and *I'm* not what *she* expected!

STEFFY   Don't you realize how nervous she was? After all these years, seeing her father for the first time. She probably didn't know what to say.

HERB   Is that so? Well, she came up with "shitheel" three times without any trouble.

STEFFY   What did you expect from her? Don't you think the girl probably has a lot of hostility stored up in her?

HERB   Well, if she felt that way, why didn't she just write me a couple of threatening letters and let it go at that?

STEFFY   Sweet-looking girl. Don't you think she's sweet-looking?

HERB   I told her that. I swear to God. She says to me, "You can't even give me a kiss." I kissed her. I felt funny about putting my arms around her. I didn't know how she would feel about it.

STEFFY   You don't have to explain it to me.

HERB   After sixteen years she just walks in here. I don't even know how she found me. It took them twenty years to find Eichmann.

STEFFY   What are you going to do?

HERB   What do you *expect* me to do? I told her she could sleep here. She's the one who walked out. Why didn't she write to me first? Or call me. Tell me she's coming out.

touch shoulder

STEFFY   Maybe she's afraid you would have said no.

HERB   That's right. I probably would have. After all these years, maybe it's better to leave things the way they were.

STEFFY   She wants to know who you are. She wants to know why you let her grow up without you. Are those unfair questions to ask, Herb?

HERB   She's interested in me for one thing, that's all. She wants me to get her into the movies. The *movies,* can you believe that? At first I thought she meant free passes.

STEFFY   Maybe saying "Get me into the movies" is just another way of saying "Let me back into your life."

HERB   What are you talking about?

STEFFY   I don't know. I'm no psychiatrist. Maybe she just wants you to do something for her to prove that you never really stopped caring.

HERB   Like getting her into the movies?

STEFFY   Yes. It's easier to ask for the impossible. When you ask for the possible, there's always the chance you'll get rejected.

HERB   When did you get so smart? You been going to UCLA on your lunch breaks?

STEFFY I've been putting make-up on insecure people for years. After a while, you get pretty good at seeing what's underneath.

HERB I can't handle her right now.

STEFFY Why not?

HERB It's a bad time for me. I'm trying to get this script finished. The thoughts don't come, the ideas aren't there. It takes me four weeks to get three words down on paper. I don't have time to start raising a daughter.

STEFFY She looks raised enough to me. I think she just wants to find out who her father is.

HERB She *knows* who it is. It's her grandmother.

STEFFY Let her stay for a couple of days. It's none of my business, Herb, but you owe her that much. She's probably still on the corner waiting for the bus.

HERB You were right before. It's none of your business.

STEFFY *(She's stopped cold)* Sorry.

HERB Steffy, why do you bother with me? I'm hardly ever nice to you. I make love to you all night and don't say two civil words to you in the morning. You're still an attractive woman. *(Peeks at a clock)* It's only nine-twenty. If you get an early start, I bet you could find someone out there who would really appreciate you.

STEFFY I thought I'd give you ten more minutes.

HERB If you can say that after two years, you're a very patient lady.

33

STEFFY   Yeah. Either that or stupid.

HERB   I see other women, you know.

STEFFY   I know. But you didn't have to tell it to me.

HERB   Well, I *am* faithful in a way. I don't tell them about *you*.

STEFFY   I don't see other men, if you're interested.

HERB   I appreciate that.

STEFFY   It's not that I don't look. I'm just not crazy about what's out there.

HERB   I know. I'm really special, right?

STEFFY   I never really ask myself what the attraction is. The truth might scare the hell out of me.

HERB   Well, I know why *you* turn me on.

STEFFY   I do too: because I'm not looking for a husband.

HERB   Noooo . . . Well, that's part of it. You turn me on because you never make any demands. You never push me. Sometimes I wonder what you would say if I really asked you to marry me.

STEFFY   I don't know. Ask me.   *challenge*

HERB   *(Laughs)* Foxy. I love foxy ladies.   *(He kisses her cheek)*   You should be a writer.

STEFFY   *(Pointedly)* So should you.   *(He turns away)* I mean it. You make me so damn furious sometimes. You've got more talent than ninety percent of the hacks in this town and you're too lazy or too scared to put it down on paper. Why won't you?

HERB   Because the other ten percent have all the jobs.

STEFFY   You know what you need? You need to have someone shove a ten-foot Roman candle up your rear end and set it off.   *slap butt*

HERB   So how come every time I ask you to do kinky stuff in bed, you always get sore at me?

STEFFY   I'm going to work.
(She picks up her purse)

HERB   Come on, give me a little smile?

STEFFY   It's impossible to have a serious discussion with you.

HERB   I'm being very serious. I would love to kiss you all over, including your pocketbook.

STEFFY   *to herself* I think I'm going to take that picture in Hawaii. Three months out of the country may do us a lot of good.

HERB   Are you kidding? You couldn't go three months without me. It's not possible.

STEFFY   Damn it, Herb. I don't like you today.

HERB   Go on, you're crazy about me.

STEFFY   I know that, but I still don't like you today. *(Starts for the door)*   Don't call me until you get five pages written. I don't care if it's lousy, I don't care if you copy it out of George Bernard Shaw, as long as it's five pages. And don't bother phoning because I won't take your calls.

HERB   Steffy! I'll call her. I'll call her today.

pause

STEFFY   Because you want to or because it's another reason to get out of working?

HERB   Probably a little of both.

STEFFY   Do you know where she is?

HERB   Yes, I know where she is.

STEFFY   Well, don't wait. You don't want a kid like that wandering around the streets. You know what can happen in this town.

HERB   *(Moving toward her, smiling)*   Last night was terrific, wasn't it? I gave you five stars in my diary.

smile

STEFFY   I still don't like you today . . . but it's very possible I can change my mind by tonight.
    (She goes out the door. He runs after her, calls out from the doorway)

HERB   Hey, Steffy! You sure make one hell of a Roman candle!

153

Blackout

SCENE 2

It is later the same evening. The house is dark. HERB *is opening the door.* LIBBY *is behind him. She carries her pack; he carries her suitcase.*

HERB   Fifteen years ago you couldn't get pastrami like that out here. Or real corned beef. They had to fly it in from New York. Thousands of hungry Jews would be waiting at the airport. *(He goes into the house. She waits outside. He looks for the wall switch)* We just got Thomas' English Muffins out here two years ago. This is still the wilderness. *(He turns on the light. Looks around)* Where is she? *(He goes to the door and looks outside)* What are you standing out there for?

LIBBY   Are you sure about this?

HERB   Fifteen bucks for dinner and a dollar and a half for parking, you think I'm fooling around?

LIBBY   You never actually invited me formally.

HERB   *Formally?* You want me to wake up a printer in the middle of the night and have something engraved?

LIBBY   All you said to me was "Get your things and let's go." I've heard the *police* say that.

HERB   Jesus! You're as difficult coming *into* a house as you are leaving it. All right. I am inviting you. You are invited into my humble abode wherein I shall make

37

you welcome with lodgings and repast and pray that your slightest wish and desire will be met most hastily and graciously.

LIBBY   I like that. That's classy.

HERB   I mean it, Libby. I'm honestly glad you're here.

LIBBY   Thanks. *(They walk in)*   I can only stay a couple of days.

HERB   What did I do now?

LIBBY   I just didn't want you getting the idea you were stuck with me for eternity.

HERB   In *California?* Don't worry. They don't give this whole place six weeks.

LIBBY   *(Looks out the window)*   How come you never see any people on the streets out here? Where is everybody?

HERB   In their cars.

LIBBY   So how do you meet anyone? What do you have to do, crash?

HERB   You meet them at red lights, filling stations. At the Motor Bureau you meet terrific people.

LIBBY   It's so quiet. Don't you miss the noise?

HERB   The refrigerator rattles in the middle of the night. It's not much but it's all I got. *(Pointing to the bed in the alcove)*   Libby, this is where you'll sleep.

LIBBY   Gee! My very own alcove. I love it . . . Do you own this house?

HERB   Me? Are you kidding? Six termites own it. They
lease it to four mice and I sublet it from them.
(She helps him make the bed)

LIBBY   Because this place could be fixed up to look real
cute. I have to be honest with you. This morning I
hated it.

HERB   It came across.

LIBBY   But it's got potential. It just needs a few touches
here and there. And it would hardly cost anything. I
can paint. I can wallpaper. I can lay bricks. I can plas-
ter.

HERB   Where did you learn to do that?

LIBBY   Back home in Brooklyn. They were going to
condemn our whole block, but the tenants got together
and fixed it up. We painted it, cleaned it up—you
couldn't recognize it. All the rats came out of the sewer,
thought they were in a rich neighborhood and moved
out to look for us.

HERB   I hope you didn't leave a forwarding address.

LIBBY   You should have seen our apartment. My bedroom looked like a night in Morocco. I painted my
ceiling midnight-blue with little stars twinkling over
my bed and a crescent moon hanging over my chest of
drawers. Robby likes London, so I painted dark clouds
on his ceiling and fog all over his walls. Would you like
something like that?

HERB   No, thanks. I'm very happy with the weather in
here.

LIBBY   Your car could use a tune-up, you know. I haven't heard coughing like that since the last flu epidemic. You got any tools? I can do it tonight.

HERB   You can tune up a car?

LIBBY   I can *make* one if I had the parts.

HERB   Terrific. Take the parts from *my* car and make me a Mercedes.

LIBBY   You think I couldn't do it?

HERB   I'm sure you can, but I couldn't afford the insurance.

LIBBY   *(Getting teabags)*   I'm making some tea. It'll be ready in a minute.

HERB   Not for me, thanks. I think I'm going to turn in.

LIBBY   You're going to sleep? We haven't even talked to each other yet.

HERB   We talked at dinner, didn't we?

LIBBY   "You want another cream soda?" is not exactly a talk. We haven't seen each other since I'm three years old. We have a lot of gaps to fill in.

HERB   Tonight? You want to fill in the entire sixteen years *tonight*?

LIBBY   Well, we could spread it out. A couple of hours every night for a week, like they did with *Roots.*

HERB   Okay. Swell. We'll start tomorrow night.

LIBBY   *(Turns away)*   Yeah. Sure. I mean, if you don't want to talk about things, I understand. If I were you, I probably wouldn't want to talk about them either.

HERB   Listen, I'll make a deal with you.

LIBBY   Yeah?

HERB   If you stop trying to make me feel guilty, I'll stop pretending I have nothing to feel guilty about.

LIBBY   I wasn't trying—

HERB   The hell you weren't.

LIBBY   Just a little.

HERB   Well, cut it out.

LIBBY   You mean I can *never* mention the fact that you walked out?
(She serves the tea)

HERB   Isn't there another way you can phrase that?

LIBBY   What? You "departed unobtrusively"?

HERB   You know, if I could write the way you talk, I'd have a house in Beverly Hills. See you in the morning.
(Going toward the bedroom)

LIBBY   I don't think so. I want to leave the house about seven.

HERB   Where are you going?

LIBBY   I thought I'd get an early start on my career. Look for an agent.

HERB   You think there are agents wandering around the streets at seven o'clock in the morning? . . . You're really serious about this, aren't you? Why, Libby? Why show business?

LIBBY   Why not?

HERB   Because you can waste your life.

LIBBY   It's my life.

HERB   You like disappointment? You like rejection?

LIBBY   I wanted to be tall. I'm not. I wanted to be skinny.
I'm not. I wanted to be gorgeous. I'm not. When you
start off your life like that, what can they do to disap-
point you?

HERB   *(Looks at her; smiles)*   Come here.   *(She goes toward him; stops a few feet away)*   All the way.   *(She
moves close to him)*   I'm sorry about this morning. I'm
sorry if we got off on the wrong foot. And I'm sorry
if I didn't give you a proper kiss—which I would like
to do right now, if it's okay with you.

LIBBY   Sure.
*(He reaches out, takes her in his arms, embraces her
and kisses her cheek. She looks disturbed)*

HERB   What's wrong?

LIBBY   Nothing. It's just a very heavy moment and I'm
trying to deal with it.

HERB   Listen, I understand how you feel. You've probably got a lot of mixed emotions. It's only natural you're
going to have a lot of hostility towards me . . . Do you?
Have a lot of hostility towards me?

LIBBY   Not a lot. Some.

HERB   Is that why you came? To let it out?

LIBBY   No . . . to get rid of it.

HERB   Thank you. I appreciate that . . . Listen, I'm going to get up at six-thirty and make you breakfast. You like waffles?

LIBBY   You can make waffles? What kind of waffles?

HERB   I don't know. I just pop 'em in the toaster. Good night, Lib.
(He goes into his room and closes the door)

LIBBY   Don't you want to see a picture of Robby?

HERB   *(Offstage)*   Who?

LIBBY   Robby! *Carl!* Your son. Don't you want to see what he looks like?

HERB   Er, yeah, sure. I didn't know you had one.
(He comes back in)

LIBBY   Well, sit down. Put your feet up. Put your slippers on. *(He sits in a chair next to a lamp)*   Do you have a pipe? I always pictured you smoking a pipe. With leather arm-patches and a couple of Great Danes. And a big library with old English books.

HERB   Who did you think I was? David Niven?

LIBBY   Yeah . . . sort of. *(He puts his glasses on)*   Anyway, here's Robby . . . or Carl . . . or whatever his name is.
(She hands him the picture. He looks at it)

HERB   Oh, he looks like a nice boy. Sweet face.

LIBBY   I think he looks a little like you.

HERB   Really? You think so? *(Looking again)* Yeah, there's a slight resemblance. He'll probably be a knockout with the girls.

LIBBY   And that's Momma . . . You still recognize her?

HERB   How could I forget her? Hasn't changed much at all . . . What has she got, blond hair now?

LIBBY   She's been through every color. Changes it every two weeks. The kids in my school thought I had fourteen different mothers.

HERB   Well, we all want to stay young, I guess.

LIBBY   And that's Grandma. I had to sit in her lap, otherwise she wouldn't smile.

HERB   She got very thin, didn't she?

LIBBY   That was when she was sick. This was about three weeks before she died. She'll give me hell tonight. She'll say I should have shown you the picture of her in Miami Beach with the suntan.

HERB   Are you going to talk to her tonight?

LIBBY   Yeah. Probably. I mean, a lot of major events have happened today. If I didn't talk to her tonight, she'd pull my pillows off the bed.

HERB   She doesn't wander around the house, does she? I'm a very light sleeper.

LIBBY   No. She just wanders around in my head.
(She goes into the bathroom)

HERB   Well, I'm going to keep my door locked, just in case. Good night, Lib.

LIBBY   Good night, Herb.
(He looks at her, then goes into his bedroom and closes the door. His door opens and he comes out)

HERB   I don't like "Herb." Can we try "Pop"?

*(She comes out of the bathroom in an oversized foot-
ball jersey)*

LIBBY Sure. Whatever you say.

HERB What's that?
(He points at her jersey)

LIBBY My nightgown.
(She goes back in)

HERB I got a boy who plays the piano and a girl who
sleeps in a football uniform. Serves me right.
*(He goes back into the bedroom and closes the door.
LIBBY takes out a paperback play from her suitcase,
opens it to a page she has marked, stands in the center of the room and begins to read aloud from the
play)*

LIBBY *(Reads sincerely but not well, using typewriter paper
as a fan)* "I expect I shall be the Belle of Amherst
when I reach my seventeenth year. I don't doubt that
I shall have perfect crowds of admirers at that age.
Then, at dances, how I shall delight to make them await
my bidding, and with what delight shall I witness their
suspense while I make my *final decision*!"
(HERB's door opens. He looks at her)

HERB Was that Grandma you were talking to?

LIBBY No. I was just practicing acting. I won't do it if
it keeps you awake.

HERB No, that's okay. I don't mind . . . How long a play
is it?

LIBBY I don't do the whole play. I just do the parts that
I like. I can whisper.

HERB   No! Don't whisper. Don't get into bad habits. If you're going to act, learn to project.

LIBBY   Okay.

HERB   Good night, Lib.

LIBBY   Good night, Pop. *(He looks at her again, and goes to his door. She turns the page and begins to read another section of the play, about twice as loud)* "THE OR-CHARD IS FULL OF BLUEJAYS. TO SEE THEM FOLLOW THE HOSE FOR A DROP OF WATER IS A TOUCHING SIGHT. THEY WON'T TAKE IT IF I HAND IT TO THEM. THEY RUN AND SHRIEK AS IF THEY WERE BEING ASSAS-SINATED. BUT OH, TO *STEAL* IT! THAT IS BLISS!" *(She looks at him)*   Too much projection?

HERB   I don't think I'm ever going to sleep unless I get something off my mind.

LIBBY   You mean, right now?

HERB   Yes. Right now.

LIBBY   Sure. What is it?
(He gets a beer from the refrigerator)

HERB   I thought you might want to know why it was I left your mother.

LIBBY   No. Not really. I mean, it's none of my business . . . Yeah, I *would* really like to know.
(She sits. Looks at him)

HERB   The truth is, I didn't like her very much . . . Oh, she was a good woman. Worked hard, never com-plained when we didn't have any money . . . The

46

trouble was, she wasn't any fun. She had no humor at all. I could never make her laugh. That's what hurt me more than anything. We'd go to a party, I'd have a couple of drinks, in an hour, I swear, I'd have them all rolling on the floor. And I'd look over at her and she'd just be staring at me. A blank look on her face. Not angry, not upset, just not understanding. As if she walked into a foreign movie that didn't have any subtitles. She just didn't know how to enjoy herself. Oh, I know where it all came from. You're poor, you grow up in the Depression, life means struggle, hard work, responsibilities. I came from the same background, but we always laughed in my house. Didn't have meat too often, but we had fun. Her father never went to a movie, never went to a play. He only danced *once* in his entire life, at his wedding—and he did *that* because it was custom, tradition, not joy, not happiness. I give him a book to read and if he found in the middle he was enjoying it, he would put it down. Education, yes. Entertainment, no . . . Anyway, we were married about four years, and one day I was just sitting there eating her mushroom and barley soup, which happened to be delicious, and I decided I didn't want any more. Not the soup—my life. So I went inside, packed my bags and said, "Blanche, I think I got to get out of here. And I don't think I'm ever coming back" . . . And I swear to you, Libby, if she had laughed I would have stayed. If she saw the craziness of what I was doing, the absurdity of it, I would have unpacked my bags and finished my soup. But she looked at me, cold as ice, and said, "If that's how you feel, who wants you?" So I put on my hat, left her whatever cash I had in my pocket, walked down the stairs and I never came back . . . And that's it. As simple as that.

LIBBY   I see. Well, how did you feel about leaving me and Robby?

HERB   I loved you. I knew I'd miss you, but I knew if I stayed you'd grow up in a house where people didn't like each other. A week later I went out to California. I was going to write to you but you were three years old. What was I going to do, draw you pictures in crayon explaining why Daddy was gone?

LIBBY   You should have written me a letter. I could have saved it. It would have been something to hold on to. I never even had a picture of you. Momma tore them all up.

HERB   She was right. I was gone, I wasn't coming back, what did you want a picture for?

LIBBY   Didn't you want one of us?

HERB   I asked your mother, she wouldn't send me one. I called a few times, she wouldn't let me speak to you. She said if I wrote, she would tear up the letters. I couldn't argue with her. She was angry, she was vindictive . . . and she was right. After a while, I pretended I didn't have kids so it wouldn't hurt so much. Then I got so good at pretending, I finally believed it. Six, seven years went by. I was working a few shows, I came to New York a couple of times, thought about calling you up . . . Then I thought it wasn't fair. She put all the time in, you were her kids. I had no right to come busting in with an armful of presents to get a kiss and a hug and then make the next plane back to California.

LIBBY   What kind of presents? You should never throw away presents.

HERB   Libby, I'm being very honest with you. I never regretted leaving her. I'm just no good at marriage . . . I know because I was married twice after that. One was a show girl, the other was a posturepedic mattress model on TV. Her name was Patty.

LIBBY   Was *she* any fun?

HERB   Oh, yeah. Terrific fun. Patty laughed at everything I said. Patty laughed at everything *anyone* said. Patty laughed in the bathtub, in the supermarket. She would laugh if the house was being carried away in a mudslide. Patty got a divorce, half my money and drove away with another guy laughing at everything *he* said.

LIBBY   Tell me about the other one.

HERB   Veronica. She was the show girl. Gorgeous body. The first year we were married, she spent seventy-one thousand dollars on clothes and jewelry. Considering I only made *fifty-eight* thousand dollars that year, I knew we had domestic problems. Six months later she was gone with the other half of my money, and when Patty heard about it, she laughed at *that* too . . . So there you are. *The Life Story of Herb Tucker,* condensed and edited for television.

LIBBY   You didn't have to tell me all that, but I'm glad you did. They say confession is good for the soul.

HERB   What do you mean, *confession?* I just left, I didn't murder the entire family.

LIBBY   You know what I mean.

HERB   Yeah. I know what you mean. I just hope you'll give me the chance to do a little better for you during the next sixteen years. Will you, Lib? Will you give me that chance?

LIBBY   You don't have to do anything. I just like listening to you talk. I like the sound of your voice.

HERB   Well, tomorrow morning, we'll have a long talk about this acting thing and all. Okay?

LIBBY   Whatever you say.

HERB   Well, I'm up. I'm never going to sleep tonight. Why don't you read me something? From one of your plays.

LIBBY   You mean *audition*? For my own father? I would have heart failure.

HERB   It's not an audition. I don't have any jobs to give you. I would just like to hear you read something.

LIBBY   *(She gets the book)*   Oh. Well, that's different. As long as I'm not on the spot here . . . This is from *The Belle of Amherst*. It's letters from the life of Emily Dickinson. Julie Harris did it on the stage. Anyway, this is one of my favorite parts. I've read it a thousand times. Are you ready?

HERB   I am ready.

LIBBY   *(Reads)*   "I dream about Father every night, always a different dream, and forget what I'm doing daytimes—wondering where he is . . . His heart was pure and terrible, and I think no other like it exists. *(They look at each other)*   I'm glad there is immortality, but would have tested it myself, before entrusting him . . . Home is so far from home—since my father died."

Curtain

SCENE I

It is two weeks later, about 7 P.M.

The bungalow has virtually been transformed. It is clean, bright and cheerful. A few inexpensive prints have been tacked on the walls. Some are modern art—a Picasso, a Braque, etc.

All the junk and refuse and old papers and magazines have disappeared from the place. The furniture has been rearranged and, in some instances, repaired. The kitchen also has been repainted, in a different and vibrant color. A seascape has been painted on the bathroom door.

HERB'*s desk has been cleared of all debris, and all that remains is his typewriter, a fresh stack of typing paper and a coffee mug filled with pens and pencils.*

LIBBY *is in a bathrobe, sitting at the typewriter at his desk. Her hair is up in curlers. She is slowly and very carefully pecking away at the keys.*

HERB *enters through the front door. The sun is just fading away. He is wearing a jacket with a folded-up racing form in his side pocket.*

LIBBY   *(Without looking up from the typewriter)*   Hi. How'd your meeting go today?

HERB   Swell. Terrific coffee and Danish.
(He looks through the mail)

LIBBY   Be careful in the bathroom. The walls aren't dry yet.

53

HERB   You didn't paint my toothbrush, did you? I was very happy with the old color.

LIBBY   No. But I changed your shower curtains. The old one looked like the one Janet Leigh was stabbed in in *Psycho*. I'm going to cut it up and make shower caps.

HERB   Just what I need. Eighty-six new shower caps. *(He puts the mail down and turns toward the kitchen)* Where's the kitchen? I don't recognize this place since you turned it into the Museum of Modern Art.

LIBBY   You can't tell me it's not cheerier in here now. It was so depressing. *Now* it looks like a happy house.

HERB   *(Getting a beer from the refrigerator)* I know. I could hear it laughing from outside. *(He goes to the window and looks out)* Hey, look how gorgeous my trees look. I think this is going to be my best year for fruit.

LIBBY   I'm using them for dinner. "Chicken à la Orange," "Salade à la Lemon"—you got anything out there I could use for dessert?

HERB   How about "Pudding à la Pits"?

LIBBY   How's the car driving now?

HERB   Perfect. I may enter the Indy 500 this year.

LIBBY   I was going to rotate the tires but I didn't have a chance yet.

HERB   How'd I get so lucky? Suddenly I have a decorator, a mechanic, a typist, a cook. They don't have that much staff on *Upstairs, Downstairs*. What are you writing?

ACT TWO

LIBBY   Letters to Mom and Robby. I told them I saw
Marlon Brando in the supermarket yesterday. My
mother'll die.

HERB   You saw Marlon Brando in the supermarket?

LIBBY   Well, someone who looked like him. You want
me to send regards to Robby?

HERB   Sure.

LIBBY   What should I say?

HERB   Say "Regards to Robby."

LIBBY   What about Mom?

HERB   What about her?

LIBBY   It would be kind of insulting to say something to
Robby and not to her.

HERB   Yeah . . . Well, say I hope she's well.

LIBBY   Is that as far as you want to go?

HERB   What else? "Sorry about that misunderstanding
sixteen years ago"? You want to write your own letters
please?

LIBBY   I was just asking.

HERB   Maybe you could say I think she did a very nice
job bringing up her daughter.

LIBBY   That's nice. She'll like that. Would you initial it
so she doesn't think I'm making it up?

HERB   Would you just type your own letters? Leave me
alone. What time is Steffy coming?

LIBBY   About seven, seven-thirty. *(She finishes typing her letter)*   So tell me what happened at the meeting. Did they like your presentation?

HERB   Yeah. Loved it. Very impressed. They feel it needs a little work, but then what doesn't?

LIBBY   But do you have a deal? A contract? Are they going to pay you?

HERB   They don't work that way. They have to okay the treatment first. They go step by step. They're very cautious out here. I'm not worried. It was a good meeting.

LIBBY   Something went wrong. They didn't like it. You're covering up something. I can tell from your voice.

HERB   You've only heard my voice for two weeks, how can you tell anything?

LIBBY   Why can't you be honest with me? I'm honest with you. I tell you everything.

HERB   What have I been dishonest about?

LIBBY   They turned down your idea and you're afraid to tell me.

HERB   They didn't turn down my idea.

LIBBY   Swear to God?

HERB   I swear to God. They didn't turn it down . . . because I didn't go to the meeting.

LIBBY   You didn't go to the meeting?

HERB   Isn't that what I just said? I called them up and canceled. I had more important things to do.

LIBBY   What did you do?

HERB   I went to the races at Hollywood Park.

LIBBY   You went to the races at Hollywood Park?

HERB   What is this, the Berlitz School of English? You don't have to repeat everything I say. I went to the races. I picked three winners. Three hundred and forty-six bucks. That's three hundred and forty-six more than I would have made if I went to that meeting today because I had nothing to give them. I came up empty, do you understand?

LIBBY   You didn't even go to the meeting?

HERB   I was not going to sit there with three teenage network executives and present them with forty-six pages of blank paper. I crapped out, okay?

LIBBY   What do you mean, forty-six empty pages? I saw you working every day for two weeks. I heard the typewriter at night. I was worried your fingers would be bleeding today.

HERB   It was no good, Libby. I didn't write forty-six pages. I wrote one page forty-six times.

LIBBY   But you said it was a good idea. Why didn't you go to the meeting? You're a terrific talker. You could have told them the idea.

HERB   Maybe seven, eight years ago. Not today. I dry up, I get nervous, I don't know what the hell I'm saying in there. You walk into a room and five smart-ass kids in Pierre Cardin suits and eighty-dollar haircuts sit there with their hands behind their heads and dare you to entertain them. I was making two grand a week, when they were pageboys at NBC. Screw 'em all when

I can make a terrific living at Hollywood Park. I'm
going to wash up.

LIBBY   You know what really gets me mad? Would you
like to know?

HERB   No.

LIBBY   What really gets me mad is when somebody stops
believing in themselves. You won't even give yourself
a break. Grandma always says to me, "You can't like
other people until you like yourself."

HERB   Really? For a woman who passed away, she cer-
tainly has a lot to say. Listen, I'm getting very antsy.
I'd like to go out tonight. Would you mind if we forget
about dinner at home? Let's go out and celebrate. You,
me and Steffy.

LIBBY   Celebrate what?

HERB   I had a very big day today. Maybe not in my line
of work, but a very big day.

LIBBY   It's up to you and Steffy. I wasn't going to be here
anyway. I'm busy tonight.

HERB   Again? That's three nights this week. You're
hardly ever home anymore.

LIBBY   Thanks. I'm glad you noticed.

HERB   Listen, it's okay with me. I want you to have a
good time . . . Where are you going?

LIBBY   It's business.

HERB   What kind of business? *Show* business?

LIBBY   I can't discuss it with you.

HERB   You discuss *my* show business, why can't we discuss *your* show business? Where do you go every night?

LIBBY   Making contacts. Is it okay if I use the car?

HERB   Why not? You built it. Listen, Libby, L.A. is a very strange place at night. If you don't know your way around, you can get in a lot of trouble. Why can't you tell me where you're going?

LIBBY   Because it's important that I do this on my own. I really appreciate your letting me stay here. If I ever thought you owed me anything, you more than paid me back. But I had a long talk with Grandma over the weekend and we decided if I'm going to make it in this business I have to do it on my own.

HERB   Grandma's still here? I thought she left. You told me she missed New York.

LIBBY   She does. But she went out to this Hillside Cemetery the other day near the airport and she met some women she used to know from Prospect Park. They moved out here when their children did and then they died. So Grandma brings them up on the news in the old neighborhood. I've got to go. If you get stuck, maybe Grandma'll help you with the dinner.
   (LIBBY *leaves through the front door*)

HERB   (*Looks up to "Grandma"*)   I'll cook. You clean up.

Blackout

It is about midnight. There is the sound of a car passing the house. HERB *comes out, wearing his robe and slippers. He seems distressed. He goes to the door and looks out.*

STEFFY *is wearing a short Japanese robe that she probably leaves there for such occasions. She stands in the doorway near the garden looking at* HERB, *sensing his distress.*

STEFFY   It's okay. I know how you feel.

HERB   You do?

STEFFY   It was a lousy day for me too. The big star came an hour and a half late and we all had to work overtime. I'm sorry if I spoiled the dinner.

HERB   You didn't spoil anything.

STEFFY   I did. I came late, the chicken was a little dry. I'm sorry.

HERB   It was timed for eight o'clock. I mean, the kid makes a chicken, baked potatoes, sour cream, chives, two vegetables and a chocolate mousse, the least you could have done was call.

STEFFY   There were twenty grips trying to get at the phone. I thought I'd make better time on the freeway.

HERB   *(Picks up a handmade card)*   She even made this beautiful little menu—"Potatoes Germaine, Peas à la Libby . . ." All the artwork she did herself. She drew

the chef's hat. She watercolored the little bunnies
around the edges—

STEFFY   It's gorgeous. I don't know what else to say.

HERB   Would you leave her a note? Would you tell her
the dinner was fantastic?

STEFFY   I'll tell her tonight. When is she coming home?
(She sits)

HERB   I don't know. She's been out there three, four
nights this week and I don't know where she is or what
she's doing. What is it now, twelve-thirty? Don't you
think that's kind of late?

STEFFY   *(Smiles)*   No. I think it's kind of wonderful.
Welcome to the World of Worried Parents. How does
it feel, Herb?

HERB   I don't like it.

STEFFY   Being a parent or being worried?

HERB   Do I get a choice?

STEFFY   Nope. It's a package deal: To love someone is to
be scared every minute of your life.

HERB   In two years with you, that was the first time I've
been preoccupied in bed. It's very hard to keep stimu-
lated while you're listening for a car to drive up.

STEFFY   For your information, it was one of the nicest
times we've had together.

HERB   Well, you're weird. I like my sex without any
distractions . . . I would call someplace, but I don't
know where to call.

61

STEFFY Interesting how worked up you're getting over a perfect stranger.

HERB What do you mean stranger? She's my daughter, isn't she?

STEFFY She's been your daughter for sixteen years but you'd need a telescope to notice it.

HERB I didn't know what she was like. She wasn't real to me. I thought she hated me. Never thought she'd want to see me. I've lived all these years and I don't know a goddamned thing about life.

STEFFY How come you only have two trees?

HERB What?

STEFFY You've got a lemon tree and an orange tree. You've got room for a few more. You got one that's dying that you don't pay any attention to . . . I was wondering why you just have two trees?

HERB I don't know what the hell you're—Oh Jesus! Don't give me that. I give up my two kids so I grow two trees. So if I left sixteen kids I'd have Yosemite National Park back there, right? I don't think we should see each other anymore, Steffy. I'm not sure it's healthy to be having sex with your analyst.

STEFFY Don't look at me. I just raised the questions, not the trees.

HERB So what's your point? Libby is my Orange and Carl is my Lemon? And their mother is the dried up one with the pits, is that it?

STEFFY I didn't mean it to be literal. I don't even know why I thought of it. I just thought of it.

HERB   And who are you? I don't see *you* growing around here.

STEFFY   *(With some resignation)*   Yeah. I don't see me growing around here either.

HERB   *(Annoyed)*   Who do you want to be? A rose? A tulip? A rhododendron? I'll get a pot and plant you tomorrow.

STEFFY   I want to be Steffy. And I want to be somebody who sees you more than whenever it just suits your fancy. I want to move on with our relationship, Herb.

HERB   *(Looks out the window)*   If she was lost, she would call me, wouldn't she?

STEFFY   What is it you're more worried about? Libby or answering my question?

HERB   What's wrong with our relationship? We've had a two-year run so far. To me, that's a big hit.

STEFFY   I lied to you a few weeks ago. I told you I don't see other men. I did. I had dinner twice with Monte Walsh—he's the cameraman on the picture. It was dinner, nothing else, but I found, much to my surprise, I enjoyed being with him. I enjoyed talking to him. I enjoyed/enjoying myself.

HERB   I'm glad. What did you have for dinner?

STEFFY   Communication.

HERB   Oh, then you must have gone to Angelo's. They make it great.

STEFFY   There's your typewriter. There's the paper. All you've got to do is get those snappy answers down on

63

the page and maybe someday *you'll* be able to afford to take *me* to Angelo's. I'm getting dressed.
(She goes into the bedroom)

HERB Jesus Christ! Two weeks ago it was peaceful around here. Now suddenly they're moving in, moving out. I'm running the goddamn Beverly Hilton.

STEFFY *(Comes out, putting on her blouse)* One daughter and one girlfriend is hardly a convention. I was hoping you could handle it.

HERB Why now? Why now after two years do you come in here and throw pressure in my face? I thought you were happy. I thought we had the perfect arrangement. I thought you *liked* being the liberated woman.

STEFFY I'm going to be forty years old in June. As a choice, liberation is terrific. As a future prospect it's a little frightening.

HERB I won't get married again.

STEFFY I don't need you to *save* me. I need you to *want* me.

HERB I'll give up seeing other women. For good. I only did it once in a while anyway. Is that what you want?

STEFFY I didn't ask you to turn this into Lent! I just want something more permanent, Herb. Not marriage, just a commitment. I've got a house twice as big as this, I've got a room for you to work in. Move in with me. No financial obligations—I make more than you do anyway. I just miss you in the mornings. I get angry because I see a perfectly good talent gathering dust on your typewriter because you're the kind of man who needs a gentle, prodding push from behind. I care and I worry about you. I don't have to be your wife, but I think I'd make a terrific pusher.

HERB   Why don't you like it the way it is anymore?

STEFFY   Nothing stays the way it is. It all changes. It moves on and there's not a damn thing you or I can do about it.

HERB   *(He's quiet. Looks away)*   I miss 1948. I played stickball on the streets from seven in the morning till six at night. A summer lasted forever. And the pennant was going to fly over Yankee Stadium for the next two hundred years.

STEFFY   I miss 1956. I wore a size-seven dress and never needed make-up. That's still not going to stop Monte Walsh from calling me tomorrow night. What do I do, Herb?

HERB   Change your number.

STEFFY   Sorry. You can't have it all your way. Not forever. When you're eighty-three and I'm seventy-seven, neither one of us is going to look forward to my coming over every Tuesday night. I put my kids on the school bus in the morning and they come home in the afternoon grown up. Don't ask me to settle for whatever it is *you're* willing to settle for. I want more for myself. I want it for *both* of us. But I'm just not going to wait around for *you* to make the decision for what *I* get.

HERB   Jesus, if it's anything I hate, it's someone who asks me to be fair. Maybe there's another way. Maybe there's some other arrangement we could make.

STEFFY   You know what I'm going to get you for Christ-
mas, Herb? An "Exit" sign. I never saw a man who
looked so hard for ways out.
*(She goes into the bedroom and returns with her skirt
and shoes)*

HERB   I got a kid missing on the streets. Can we talk
about this tomorrow?

STEFFY   She's not missing. She's just *out* . . . All right,
we'll talk about it tomorrow.
(She puts her skirt on)

HERB   I *know* this place is a dump. I *know* I should get
out of here. But it's just not that easy. I feel "comfortable" here.

STEFFY   Your lucky house?

HERB   Maybe it's what I think I deserve—"The House
That Guilt Built."
pleading, pull on him
STEFFY   Listen, we could take the trees with us. I know
a guy who does great transplants. I have apples and
pears. With your oranges and lemons, we'd make great
fruit salad.
*(HERB looks at her warmly. She puts her arms around
him and embraces him)*

HERB   Monte Walsh, heh?

STEFFY   Sorry . . . How does it make you feel?

HERB   Angry. Competitive. Scared. I've seen him
around. Wears a cowboy hat, always looks like he's in
Marlboro Country. What kind of cologne does he
wear? Sagebrush?

STEFFY He makes me smile but he's never made me laugh.

HERB Yeah? Well, the bastard's making me nervous.

STEFFY I know the feeling. That's what Libby's doing to me.

HERB Libby?

STEFFY (*Gets her shoes and starts putting them on*) It's tough for a woman you've known for two years to compete with a daughter you haven't seen in sixteen.

HERB Are you crazy? What's Libby got to do with you and me?

STEFFY Don't ask me. I didn't make up nature.

HERB I don't understand you. I don't understand women. To tell you the truth, I don't trust *anyone* who can't go to deep center field and catch a fly ball.

STEFFY You know me. I say what's on my mind. She's got something I wish I had.

HERB What?

STEFFY *You* worrying about where I am at twelve-thirty.

HERB I *know* where you are. You're in the living room putting your clothes on instead of in the bedroom taking them off. Don't give me deadlines, Steffy. Don't tell me I have to make a decision this week. You want to have dinner with Monte Walsh, have dinner with him. You want to hunt buffalo with him, have a good time. See him as much as you want. I've got a script I not only have to finish, I have to *start*. I've got a daughter

67

who wants to be a movie star by Sunday morning and I've got a dead grandmother in Brooklyn watching every move I make—that's all I can handle right now. You want a happy ending, you'll have to come up with it yourself.

STEFFY   I'm not dumb enough to look for happy endings. I'd gladly settle for a promising middle.

HERB   I'm sorry, Stef. I used up all my promises for this week.

STEFFY   *(Nods, knowing there's no use pushing)*   Sure. Forget it. I just thought I'd mention it in passing. *(She goes into the bedroom and gets her purse)*

HERB   *(He looks out the window)*   It looks cold out. I wonder if she's dressed warmly enough.

STEFFY   She walked over the Rocky Mountains in shorts, she'll get through Wilshire Boulevard in a Mustang.

HERB   How much do I owe her?

STEFFY   For what?

HERB   For waiting sixteen years before I started worrying if she's dressed warmly enough?

STEFFY   I don't know. The minute you think you owe somebody something, you start paying them back for the wrong reasons. Forget the sixteen years, you can't make them up. In a way you're lucky. If you never left, she'd be nineteen years old anyway and still resent you for being a parent. I don't miss a breakfast with my kids and I'm going to end up in the same place you are.

68

HERB You know what? You're one of the smartest ladies
I know. *helpless — take his hand*

STEFFY Then how come I'm going home alone at
twelve-thirty at night?

HERB You're just dumb when it comes to picking men.
*(They stand there and look at each other, both feeling
a little helpless. The lights fade and go to black)*

44

SCENE 3

It is a little after 3 A.M. One lamp is on. The headlights of a car hit the house as it drives up. The car lights go off; we hear a door slam. LIBBY *enters the house and closes the door very gently. She starts to tiptoe quietly towards her room.* HERB *is sitting on the couch watching her.*

HERB   What's the point in tiptoeing? You could hear the car pull up in Denver.

LIBBY   *(Softly)*   I didn't want to wake you.

HERB   You have to fall asleep before someone can wake you.

LIBBY   *(Softly)*   Why didn't you take your pill?

HERB   I *took* a pill. The pill is more worried about you than *I* am.

LIBBY   *(Softly)*   I'm sorry. I thought you'd be busy doing other things.

HERB   I *did* other things. What are you whispering for?

LIBBY   I don't want to wake Steffy.

HERB   She's not that light a sleeper. She went home two hours ago.
(He puts on the lights)

LIBBY   How come? Doesn't she usually stay over?

HERB   *(Edgy)*   Well, she's not usually staying over to-night.

70

LIBBY   What's wrong? Anything happen with you two?

HERB   Never mind Steffy. How about explaining where you've been till three o'clock in the morning?

LIBBY   I was out.

HERB   What do you mean, "out"? Three nights this week you come home two, two-thirty, three o'clock, I want to know where you've been.

LIBBY   I'm okay. I'm fine. What are you getting so huffy about?

HERB   *Huffy?* You walk out of here, don't tell me where you're going, you don't call, you don't know anybody in this city, you walk in three o'clock in the morning and you don't think I have a right to be *huffy*?

LIBBY   *(Shrugs)*   You want to be huffy, be huffy.

HERB   Don't test me! Don't play games with me! If you think I'm going to keep paying through the nose for the sixteen years I owe you, you've got another guess coming. It's a bad debt. Forget it. You're never going to collect.

LIBBY   All I asked you for is one lousy introduction to some of your big-shot friends. Which I never got because you don't have.

HERB   You've been on my back asking for payoffs ever since you walked in here with that Orphan Annie look on your face. "You owe me and I'm here to collect"— that's what you said to me. *(Looks up)* Am I right, Grandma? Am I making that up? You're my witness. Is she listening now or do I have to dial an unlisted number?

LIBBY   Boy oh boy, *something* happened tonight.

HERB   I'm waiting for an answer.

LIBBY   I was out meeting people.

HERB   *What* people?

LIBBY   Important people . . . in the business.
(*She munches casually on a chicken leg throughout*)

HERB   *Show* business?

LIBBY   That's right.

HERB   I see. And what important people in show business did you meet tonight?

LIBBY   Producers, directors, actors . . .

HERB   Really? Anyone I might know?

LIBBY   I don't know if you *know* them, you may have *heard* of them.

HERB   Like who?

LIBBY   Like Jack Nicholson.

HERB   Jack Nicholson? . . . Yes, I've heard of him. You met him tonight?

LIBBY   That's right.

HERB   I see. Who else did you meet?

LIBBY   In movies or in television?

HERB   Either one.

LIBBY   James Caan.

HERB   Oh? You met "Jimmy"? How is he?

LIBBY   He looked terrific to me.

HERB   I'm sure he did. Anyone else I might have heard of?

LIBBY   Let me see . . . Candice Bergen, Suzanne Pleshette, someone who's a vice-president at Columbia
Pictures, that director who directed *Jaws* . . . A lot of
others, I can't remember their names.

HERB   Well, you must have been so busy. Did you talk
to these people?

LIBBY   Sure. I mean, we didn't have major conversations
but I talked to them.

HERB   *(Looks at her)*   You mean the way you talk to
Grandma?

LIBBY   No. Grandma's dead. These people were all
dressed up. I know the difference.

HERB   I'm just asking. And where did you meet "Jack"
and "Jimmy" and "Candy"?

LIBBY   At a party in Beverly Hills—11704 Benedict Can-
yon.

HERB   Who invited you?

LIBBY   Gordon Zaharias.

HERB   *Gordon Zaharias?* Who the hell is Gordon Zaharias?

LIBBY   He's the one who got me the job.

HERB   *What* job?

73

LIBBY   Parking cars at the party in Beverly Hills. I made thirty-two dollars plus tips—not including meeting Jack Nicholson.

HERB   That's where you met all these people? Parking their cars?

LIBBY   Well, for a while I was just the relay man. Like, George Segal would come out and say, " '78 Blue Mercedes." Then I would run like crazy down the hill and yell to this other guy, " '78 Blue Mercedes" and he would get to drive it up. But then I gave him ten dollars plus half my tips so I could get to drive the car up and meet George Segal. He was very nice. He smiled and said, "Thanks," just like in *A Touch of Class.* I made a lot of great contacts.

HERB   George Segal saying "Thanks" is what you consider making a good contact?

LIBBY   Well, it doesn't hurt. The important thing was leaving the cards on the windshield.

HERB   What cards?

LIBBY   Well, we had to leave this little card that says, "Sunset Valet Parking—No Party Is Too Big or Too Small." Only, on the back of each card I wrote, "Libby Tucker, New York trained actress—No Part Is Too Big or Too Small." With my phone number. I must have left thirty of them. Even if only two people call, it was worth the money I spent.

HERB   (*Looks at her, then looks away, trying to figure her out*) Libby, can I ask you a serious personal question? Do you honestly believe that anybody in this business—a director, a producer, a cameraman, *anybody*—is going to call someone for an audition because they left their name on the *back* of a valet parking ticket?

LIBBY Not a *big* chance. But a better chance than if I left nothing at all.

HERB YOU HAVE *NO* CHANCE! NONE! There are five thousand qualified agents in this town who can't get their clients a meeting with these people but *you* think they're going to call *you* because *you* left *your* name on the back of a stub they're going to throw out the window the minute they pull out of the driveway?

LIBBY That's a very pessimistic attitude to take.

HERB *(Trying to control himself)* Okay! For the sake of argument, let us say someone looks at the card. Someone is looking for a valet service for his son's bar mitzvah. Someone just met a girl at the party and wants to write down her number. Someone has a piece of spare rib in his teeth and is trying to pick it out with the card. Only a small percentage of *that* group will look at the *back* of the card. But let's say one does. He sees, "Libby Tucker, New York trained actress—No Part Is Too Big or Too Small." Do you imagine he's going to slam his foot on the brake, pull off the road and say to his wife, "That's exactly what I'm looking for. An actress trained in New York who doesn't if her part is too big or too small. Right under my nose in my very own car. What a break for me. I'll contact her first thing in the morning and hope and pray that someone else with spare ribs in their teeth didn't get to her before me!"

LIBBY *(Shakes her head)* With an attitude like that, I can see why you don't get too much done.

75

HERB   Forget I mentioned it. I'm sorry I brought it up. I'll stay out of this room tomorrow morning in case you're swamped with phone calls.
(He starts for his bedroom)

LIBBY   If I stayed in Brooklyn, I never would have come out here. If I never came out here, I never would have met Steffy. If I didn't meet Steffy, she never would have told me about the Los Angeles Academy of Dramatic Arts. If I didn't go over to the Los Angeles Academy of Dramatic Arts, I never would have met Gordon Zaharias of Peoria, Illinois. If I didn't meet Gordon Zaharias, I never would have gotten a job driving George Segal's car. If I didn't drive all those big shots' cars, the name and number of Libby Tucker would never be stuck in their windshields. Where is *your* number stuck? If you don't pick yourself up and do something in this world, they bury you in Mount Hebron Cemetery and on your tombstone it says, "Born 1906—Died 1973 . . . and in between HE DIDN'T DO NOTHIN' "!

HERB   *(Losing his temper)*   Leaving cards in windshields is *not* how you become an actress.

LIBBY   And going to Hollywood Park Racetrack is not how you get a script written.

HERB   Don't you tell me what to do! I haven't asked you for your advice or your help.

LIBBY   And I stopped asking for yours. I'm an independently self-employed woman!

HERB   You're a dreamer, that's what you are. You paint Morocco on your ceiling and pretend you don't live in Brooklyn. You pretend your father is the King of Hollywood and you're going to march out here and become the Princess. Well, life isn't pretending. It's goddamned hard work.

(He goes into his bedroom)

LIBBY *(Calls out)* Sorry! *(He reenters)* I'm sorry. I didn't mean to get you upset. I thought you'd be pleased with how well things are going for me.

HERB I don't know. Maybe you're right. Maybe sheer determination is all you need. Are you going to be parking any more cars this week?

LIBBY Saturday night in Beverly Hills. There's a big party.

HERB Well, if it's not too much trouble, mention me on one of your cards. See you in the morning.

(He goes into his bedroom. She watches after him, then goes to his door)

ND Scene

LIBBY I was wondering if I could discuss something else with you.

HERB *(Offstage)* I just took my pill.

LIBBY It's kind of an emergency. It's something that came up tonight and I'm not sure I know how to handle it.

HERB *(Offstage)* My eyes are starting to close.

LIBBY Yeah. Okay. Never mind. I'll try to work it out for myself. Good night.

HERB *(Comes out)* Would you *stop doing that!* Okay, what's it about?

LIBBY Sex!

HERB   Sex?

LIBBY   Don't get nervous. If you get nervous, I'll get nervous.

HERB   What do you mean, sex?

LIBBY   *(Shrugs)*   Sex! Things that have to do with things sexual.

HERB   Are you in any kind of trouble?

LIBBY   Yeah. I think so.

HERB   What kind of trouble?

LIBBY   I don't know how to do anything sexual.

HERB   *That's* the trouble you're in?

LIBBY   Most of the people left the party. And Gordon and I were sitting at the bottom of the hill in Suzanne Pleshette's car. And he wanted to fool around. He's not gorgeous but he's kinda cute. And I felt very grateful to him, and I didn't want to hurt his feelings. And I wanted to fool around too. Only I didn't know what was right. I didn't want to be one of those girls they call "easy," but I didn't want to be impossible either. So I just kissed him and got out of the car and decided not to deal with it. But this Saturday night I think I'm going to have to deal with it.

HERB   And you want to discuss this with me?

LIBBY   It doesn't have to be this minute. But Sunday morning'll be too late.

HERB   You never talked about these things with your mother?

LIBBY   She doesn't trust men too much. You can guess why.

HERB   What about your grandmother?

LIBBY   Well, sex isn't her best subject. I brought it up a couple of times but she pretended she was dead.

HERB   Are you telling me that you don't know the first thing about sex?

LIBBY   No. I know how it works. I don't have any mechanical problems. I've seen five X-rated movies. I could pass a test on it. I just don't know what to expect —emotionally.

HERB   I see. Would you feel more comfortable talking to Steffy about it?

LIBBY   Probably. But it's more important I talk to you.

HERB   Why?

LIBBY   Because you're my father. And what you think means a lot to me.

HERB   That's a very nice thing to say. I appreciate that.

LIBBY   If it's a major trauma for you, I understand. I mean, I could always take a couple of glasses of wine and just plunge in.

HERB   You're not plunging into anything. I'd just like to know, is Gordon, what's-his-name, important enough to be the first time in your life?

LIBBY   It's got to be the first time sometime. If it's not him, I could always use the information.

HERB   You know what you are, Libby? Unique. Uni-quest kid I ever met . . . I don't know where to start this thing.

LIBBY   Should I ask you some questions?

HERB   Good idea. Ask me some questions.

LIBBY   Like what?

HERB   How do I know? I have to hear the questions.

LIBBY   Well . . . Emotionally, is it different for the man than it is for the girl?

HERB   Is it different for the man than it is for the girl? . . . Yes!

LIBBY   It *is*?

HERB   Am I wrong?

LIBBY   This isn't a test. I just want to know the answer. How old were you the first time?

HERB   Fifteen.

LIBBY   FIFTEEN?

HERB   I grew up in a tough neighborhood. A fifteen-year-old virgin was considered gay.

LIBBY   Who was the girl?

HERB   I didn't notice. It was very dark and I just wanted to get it over with.

LIBBY   What was it like with Mom? . . . That's a very personal question, isn't it?

HERB   So far it tops the list . . . Well, she was different from anyone I had ever met before. She was respectable. I liked that. Her family had *Time* magazine on the table—to me, that was cultured.

LIBBY   Did you do it with her before or after you were married?

HERB   I didn't think you could top the other question. What did she say?

LIBBY   She said after.

HERB   She did? . . . Yeah. We did it after.

LIBBY   No, you didn't. I knew she lied. She just couldn't talk to me about those things. That's why I'm talking to you. I wanted to know how she felt. If she was scared or excited. Was it fun? Was it painful? I didn't think it was an unreasonable question. I mean, if she could teach me how to walk, why couldn't she teach me how to love?

HERB   I don't know.

LIBBY   So what was she like? Making love.

HERB   Libby, there's just so much I can handle.

LIBBY   Because she was so angry when you left. So bitter. I don't think she ever slept with another man after you were gone.

HERB   You never can tell. She's not unattractive.

LIBBY   It's like when you left, you took her with you. That's why I was so angry with you. It was bad enough you were gone, but you could have left my mother there for me.

HERB   She *was* there for you. Look, if she didn't see other men, that was *her* choice. Maybe *you* were the other men in her life.

LIBBY   Yeah. No wonder I grew up to be a fruitcake.

HERB   Don't talk like that.

LIBBY   She used to hug me so hard sometimes. Like she was trying to squeeze all the love out of me that she wasn't getting anywhere else. So instead of growing up to be me, I grew up to be a substitute—

HERB   You're no substitute. You're first-string all the way. I never saw a girl your age who was so sure of herself. Jesus, if I had *half* your confidence, maybe you'd have been parking *my* car at that party tonight.

LIBBY   Confidence? . . . I'm scared from the minute I wake up every morning.

HERB   Of what?

LIBBY   Of everything. I get up an hour before you just to check if you're still there . . . I know Grandma's dead. I know she probably can't hear me. But I speak to her every day anyway because I'm not so sure anyone else is listening. If I have to go for an interview, my heart pounds so much you can see it coming through my blouse. That thing about writing my name on the valet stubs? It wasn't my idea. It was Gordon's. He did it first, so I just copied him . . . If you want the God's honest truth, I don't even want to be an actress. I don't know the first thing about acting. I don't know *what* I want to be . . . *(Beginning to break down)*   I just wanted to come out here and see you. I just wanted to know what you were like. I wanted to know why I was so frightened every time a boy wanted to reach out and touch me . . . I just wanted somebody in the family to hold me because it was *me*, Libby, and not somebody who wasn't there . . .

(She is sobbing. He quickly reaches out and grabs her in his arms)

HERB   I'm here, baby, I'm here. It's all right. Don't cry. I'm holding you, baby, I'm holding you.
(He cradles her in his arms as she sobs silently)

LIBBY   Don't let go yet . . . please.

HERB   You can stay in my arms as long as you like. You can move in tonight—put all your clothes in my pockets.

LIBBY   I love Mom so much. I didn't mean to say anything against her.

HERB   I know that.

LIBBY   It's just that she won't let me inside. When she holds me, all I can feel is her arms . . . but I never feel what's inside.

HERB   I understand.

LIBBY   *(Crying openly now; turns away)*   Boy oh boy . . . Really opened up the old waterworks. I never expected to do that. I hope you have flood insurance.

HERB   Libby. It can also be wonderful.

LIBBY   What can?

HERB   Giving yourself to someone . . . loving them, giving them pleasure, making them happy . . . making yourself happy. It's that way with me and Steffy. Every time. Haven't missed yet.

LIBBY   Really?

HERB   I wouldn't lie to you.

LIBBY   Then why do you only ask her to come over once a week?

HERB   You're not the only one with shaky confidence. *(They embrace as the lights fade to black)*

82

SCENE 4

It is Sunday morning, a few days later, about 11 A.M.

HERB *(Coming out of the bedroom and calling toward the bathroom)* Libby? You up? C'mon, we're going to Nate and Al's for breakfast. I want a mushroom and onion omelette, bagels, cream cheese and a pot of hot coffee. We're going to the Dodger game. I got tickets yesterday. Dodgers. Phillies. *(He looks out into the garden)* What a gorgeous day. Nice and cloudy. You know what I was thinking? Maybe you could make a sunroof for the car? I mean, it's ready to fall in anyway, it shouldn't be too big a job. What do you think? *(LIBBY emerges, wearing her original outfit)* Is that what you're going to wear? We're not going to *hike* to Dodger Stadium . . . You don't look too happy. You don't want to go to the game? It's okay. You don't have to go. I just thought you might enjoy it.

LIBBY *(Tentatively)* I would. I would really love to go with you.

HERB So why the long face?

LIBBY It's not a long face . . . It's a goodbye face. I'm going home.
(She begins to tie on her hiking boots)

HERB What do you mean?

LIBBY I mean, I'm going back home. To New York.

HERB When?

85

LIBBY Today. Now. I was waiting for you to get up. I called Steffy to say goodbye. She said she would try to get over before I left.

HERB You mean for good?

LIBBY I hope not. I hope you'll invite me to come out again sometime . . . I hope you'll come out to visit me in New York. I hope I'll have my own place by then. Maybe you can sleep in *my* alcove.

HERB When did you decide all this?

LIBBY Last night. I couldn't sleep. I was lying in bed and suddenly I heard a voice say to me, "Libby, it's time to go home. You got what you came for." And I suddenly realized it wasn't Grandma's voice. It was mine. So I got up this morning and packed my bags.

HERB What do you mean you got what you came out for? What did you get? A job parking cars? Is that what this whole trip was for?

LIBBY No. It was to get something from you. I thought it was a career or maybe just to tell you that I thought you were a shitheel. But the other night when you held me in your arms and said I could stay there as long as I wanted, I could feel your heart beating, I could feel what was *inside*—and I knew then, when you were holding me, that that's what it was I came out for.

HERB Then why do you have to go back? Why now? It took us sixteen years to get to this place. It doesn't seem right to go back the way we were.

LIBBY We're not going back the way we were. I'm just going back to New York. We have a relationship now.

I know who you are; you know who I am. That's a whole new place for us.

HERB What's in New York for you? What are you going to do there?

LIBBY Start to think about what I want to do with my life instead of wasting my time being angry with what I didn't get.

HERB But you just got here. A couple of lousy weeks, what's that? Stay a month, two more weeks. Go to the Dodger game with me, Libby. Don't go home today. Please . . . Jesus. I'm just going to miss you so damn much.

LIBBY We can call each other. We can write. I always imagined you wrote the most wonderful letters, being a professional and all. I'll save them up and make a book out of them. You know, like Groucho Marx's letters to his son.

HERB "The Post Cards of Herbert Tucker."

LIBBY That's not a bad title.

HERB You'll need money for the plane.

LIBBY I saved it. I made a lot this week. I'm going to take the bus to Chicago and hitch the other half.

HERB You're not going to hitch. *(Reaching for his wallet)* Here's some money.

LIBBY No, Daddy. I don't want it. Please.

HERB It was worth it just to hear you call me Daddy. Christ, I think I would have been better off if you never came.

LIBBY Don't say that.

HERB Well, I'm mad, damn it. I'm pissed off at you. You could have given me some warning. If I knew you were only going to stay two weeks, I never would have—

LIBBY What?

HERB Never mind.

LIBBY You never would have what? Gotten so attached?

HERB I didn't say that.

LIBBY But you were going to . . . Why couldn't you say it? What is it about attachments that scares you so much?

HERB Unattachments.

LIBBY Listen. You want to go to the game, I'll go to the game. I can leave tomorrow.

HERB No. What's the point? I'll give the tickets to Steffy's kids.
(He sits and holds his stomach with a grimace)

LIBBY What's wrong? Are you all right?

HERB I just have an empty feeling in my stomach— maybe I'm hungry.

LIBBY You're not going to go back to not eating again, are you? Not taking care of yourself? I'm going to mail you sandwiches every day from New York.

HERB Mail them early in the morning. I can't stand cold pastrami.

LIBBY   These have been the best two weeks of my life. I wouldn't have traded them for anything.
(STEFFY *appears at the door*)

STEFFY   I ran out of gas two blocks away. I was afraid I'd miss you. Oh God, am I out of shape.

LIBBY   It looks plenty good to me. Doesn't it look good to you, Dad?
(HERB *gets up and goes into the garden*)

STEFFY   How does he feel about your leaving?

LIBBY   Terrible. Isn't it wonderful?

STEFFY   You look different than that first day you got here. Taller. Did you get taller?

LIBBY   Yeah. Inside. I also got gorgeous but it didn't come out yet.

STEFFY   You could have fooled me. Oh. This is for you.
(*She hands her a manila envelope*)

LIBBY   What is it?

STEFFY   It's a present. Open it.
(LIBBY *opens it and takes out an eight-by-ten glossy photograph of Jane Fonda*)

LIBBY   "To Libby . . . From what I hear, a girl after my own heart. Best wishes, Jane Fonda." Well, that did it. You have just destroyed a tall, gorgeous girl from Brooklyn. In two weeks everything I ever wanted came true. This is some place to live.
(LIBBY *goes to her knapsack on the coffee table and puts the picture in it*)

STEFFY   I almost got Candice Bergen's for you too.

LIBBY   Oh that's okay. I know Candice. We already met.
(HERB *comes in from the garden with three oranges in
his hand. He goes to the kitchen, and puts them into
a bag*)

HERB   Here's some oranges. You ought to take some
oranges to eat on the trip.

LIBBY   Jeez. I forgot to tell Mom I'm coming home. Dad?
Can I call long distance? I'll pay you back.
(LIBBY *rushes to the phone and dials*)

STEFFY   Should I wait outside?

LIBBY   No. Stay. It's okay. *(Into the phone)*   Hello,
Mom? . . . Hi, Mom. It's me. Libby . . . No. Everything's terrific . . . How are you? . . . Your feet are
bothering you? . . . Well, don't stand on them so much
. . . *(Hand over the phone, to* STEFFY*)*   She says, "So
what should I stand on?" *(Back into the phone)*
Mom? Listen. I just wanted to tell you I'm coming
home . . . I'm leaving today . . . No, no, no—things are
wonderful. I'll tell you all about it when I get there
. . . Well, I've missed you too . . . I think about you all
the time . . . There's so many things I want to talk to
you about now . . . I've become very enlightened in
California . . . *Enlightened* . . . Forget it, I'll explain it
Wednesday . . . Listen, Mom, could you hold on for
one second? Don't go away.   *(She puts her hand over the
phone. To* HERB*)*   You don't have to say yes. I know
it's an imposition, but it would mean an awful lot to me
. . . Would you say hello to her?

HERB   Libby!

LIBBY   It doesn't have to be a conversation. Just a plain
hello. She's feeling kind of low. I can hear it in her

voice. It would be a nice gesture—with Mother's Day coming up in three weeks.

HERB What's the matter with you, Libby? I haven't spoken to the woman in sixteen years. You don't just pick up a phone and say hello.

LIBBY It's only the first few seconds that's hard.

HERB Don't do this to me, Libby. Don't do this to your mother. It's embarrassing for both of us.

LIBBY I'm not trying to make a *match*. I just thought it would be nice if everybody didn't spend the rest of their lives hung up on something that happened sixteen years ago.

HERB Steffy, would *you* please explain it to her!

LIBBY Let me ask Mom. If she says okay, will you say okay?

HERB She's not going to say okay. Why would she say okay?

LIBBY She might surprise you. You never know. Can I ask her?

HERB Go ahead. Ask her. I know the woman.

LIBBY *(Into the phone)* Mom? There's somebody here who wants to say hello to you . . . Yeah. He's standing right here . . . How do you feel about it? . . . Uh-huh . . . Uh-huh . . . All right, wait a minute. *(Hand over the phone, she moves toward HERB)* She says if you would like to say hello, she won't stop you.

HERB You see! What did I tell you?

LIBBY That's a *yes*! She said yes.

91

HERB   *That's the worst "yes" I ever heard!*

LIBBY   She's waiting on the phone. If you don't say hello *now,* that would *really* be a lousy thing to do.

HERB   *(He glares at her)*   You're something! You're really something! Two more weeks of you and *I* would have hitchhiked back to New York.   *(He goes toward her)*   Gimme the phone!

LIBBY   *(Into the phone)*   MOM? . . . Here's—him.
(She hands him the phone. He takes it and looks around despairingly)

STEFFY   I have to wash my hands.
(She goes into the bathroom)

LIBBY   I have to make your bed.
(She goes into his room and closes the door. HERB is alone. He looks at the phone, takes a deep breath and plunges in)

HERB   Hello? . . . Blanche? . . . It's Herb . . . Yeah . . . Yeah, it's a surprise for me too . . . How have you been? . . . Oh? . . . Yeah, well, I have trouble with my feet sometimes too . . . Libby showed me a picture of you. You looked very well . . . You were wearing a blue dress with an orange sweater . . . No. You didn't look heavy at all . . . You looked the same as ever to me . . . The thing I wanted to say was . . . Well, I think Libby's a terrific kid . . . A little outspoken, you know, but er . . . Well, you did a wonderful job with her, Blanche, and you should be very proud . . . Very, very proud . . . Yes. Well, it was nice talking to you too . . . Take care of yourself, Blanche . . . Who? . . . Sure. Sure, if he's there, put him on . . . *(He waits, takes another deep breath)* Hello? Hello, Robby, how are you? . . . Well, it's nice meeting you too . . . I hear you play the piano . . . You like it? . . . Yeah, I like it. It's a nice instrument . . . What's that? . . . Yeah. Yeah, I'm working on a script right now, as a matter of fact . . . Oh, you saw that one? That was about three years ago . . . I'm glad you liked it . . . I didn't know you saw it . . . No kidding? Really? Well, if you do, you just look me up . . . Your sister has the address . . . Okay. I have to go too . . . It was good speaking to you . . . Say goodbye to your mother . . . Goodbye, Robby. *(He cries a moment; then)* . . . You can come out now!

> *(Both* STEFFY *and* LIBBY *come out at exactly the same time)*

LIBBY   Thank you. That was very nice what you said about me. What'd you think of Robby?

HERB   He didn't sound like a Carl. He has a very high voice, hasn't he?

LIBBY   It gets that way when he gets nervous. Don't worry. He's not what you're thinking.

HERB   Who said anything? He may come out here next summer. He may go to school out here. He said he'd like to come by and see me.

LIBBY   You see! You see! Now aren't you glad you said "Hello"?

HERB   I suppose this means your mother comes out the summer after Robby.

LIBBY   No. You'd never get Mom out of her apartment. She'll live in Brooklyn until the day she dies, and then they'll bury her next to Grandma.

HERB Then starts the three-way conversations. You'll have to put in another line.

STEFFY I'm leaving now too. I can drop you off wherever you want.

LIBBY No, thanks. I want to leave the way I came. On my own. A girl has to be independent these days. Have I got everything?

HERB The fruit. Don't forget your fruit.

LIBBY *(Looks at them)* Thanks. You really grow great oranges and lemons.

STEFFY I'm sure glad this was the right Herb Tucker you were looking for that morning.

LIBBY Listen, if you ever do a picture in New York, we have a spare room for you. It used to be Grandma's. I did it over in French Riviera.

STEFFY I *love* French Riviera. I have to wash my hands again.
    (She goes into the bathroom)

LIBBY Sooo . . . Here it is again. Another one of those goodbye days.

HERB *(Looks around)* I feel like I should be giving you something more to take with you . . . I don't know what else to give you.

LIBBY I can think of something.

HERB You can? What?

LIBBY Your picture.

HERB My picture? *(He looks around)* Gee, I don't know if I have any good ones. *(Opens drawers)* I

had some publicity shots but they're about six years old.
I had a mustache. It doesn't even look like me.
(LIBBY *takes out a Kodak Instamatic*)

LIBBY   I came all prepared. All you have to do is stand
there.

HERB   Oh, God. I hate taking pictures.

LIBBY   You're not. *I'm* taking it. You're just posing.
(She focuses the camera. He poses uncomfortably)   Can't
you do something? You look like you're being booked
for prison.

HERB   What do you want me to do? Dance on the ceiling?

LIBBY   No. Just give me a smile. Come on. Force yourself. That's a smile? That's how they look at Mount
Hebron Cemetery. A big smile for Libby, okay?   *(He
smiles. She snaps)*   Stay there! One more for Robby.
(He smiles. She snaps)   And one for Mom.

HERB   Oh, come on.

LIBBY   For Mother's Day. Be a sport.   *(He smiles. She
snaps)*   Thank you. The rest I'm going to use for
America. Well, I think I'm going to go very quickly
because in five more minutes I'm going to take root and
grow into a New York apple tree . . . Goodbye, Daddy.
I love you.
(LIBBY *runs out the door. The bathroom door opens
and* STEFFY *comes out)*

STEFFY   Well, I think I'll be going myself. Would it be
all right if I borrow your car for a few minutes? I have
to pick up a can of gasoline. I'll be right back.

HERB   Sure.

STEFFY   I was going to take in a picture with the kids, and a Chinese dinner. You interested?

HERB   I don't know. I thought I might get a few pages done today.

STEFFY   On a Sunday?

HERB   The typewriter doesn't know. It could be Wednesday to him.

STEFFY   Sure. Well, maybe some other time.

HERB   Yeah.

STEFFY   You got something you're working on?

HERB   Yeah. I think so.

STEFFY   I'm glad to hear it . . . Something new?

HERB   No. It's an old idea. Actually, it came to me about sixteen years ago.

STEFFY   I like it already.   *(She turns and goes to the car.* HERB *goes to his desk and sits.* STEFFY *returns)*   I forgot the keys . . . I see you've gone in for advertising.

HERB   What?
            *(*STEFFY *hands him a small red card)*

STEFFY   That was on your steering wheel.   *(She hands the card to* HERB. *He reads it, smiles and hands it back to* STEFFY, *who reads it aloud)*   "Herbert Tucker. New York trained writer. No script too big or too small."

Curtain

Since 1960, a Broadway season without a Neil Simon comedy or musical has been a rare one. His first play was *Come Blow Your Horn*, followed by the musical *Little Me*. During the 1966–67 season *Barefoot in the Park, The Odd Couple, Sweet Charity* and *The Star-Spangled Girl* were all running simultaneously; in the 1970–71 season, Broadway theatergoers had their choice of *Plaza Suite, Last of the Red Hot Lovers* and *Promises, Promises*. Next came *The Gingerbread Lady, The Prisoner of Second Avenue, The Sunshine Boys, The Good Doctor, God's Favorite, California Suite, Chapter Two,* the musical hit *They're Playing Our Song,* and the new comedy *I Ought to Be in Pictures*.

Mr. Simon began his writing career in television, writing *The Phil Silvers Show* and Sid Caesar's *Your Show of Shows*. He has also written for the screen: the adaptations of *Barefoot in the Park, The Odd Couple, Plaza Suite, The Prisoner of Second Avenue, The Sunshine Boys, California Suite,* and most recently, *Chapter Two*. Other original screenplays he has written include *The Out-of-Towners, The Heartbreak Kid, Murder By Death, The Goodbye Girl, The Cheap Detective* and *Chapter Two*.

The author lives in California and New York with his actress wife, Marsha Mason. He has two daughters, Ellen and Nancy.